1966

MAMMON AND THE BLACK GODDESS

MAMMON AND THE BLACK GODDESS

by

ROBERT GRAVES

Doubleday & Company, Inc., Garden City, New York

1965

Foreword

Mammon and the Black Goddess of Wisdom are deities standing in such extreme opposition that they provide a convenient title for these eight wide-ranging pieces: all of which, with the exception of *Real Women*, began as lectures. Since what pleases the ear is usually too diffuse for the eye, I have now tightened the arguments. Their original occasions are listed in the Table of Contents; and I thank the City College of New York University for allowing me, under the Jacob C. Saposnehov Memorial Bequest, to repeat *Mammon*, *Moral Principles in Translation*, and *Intimations of the Black Goddess*. The three Oxford Lectures on Poetry were published in *Horizon*.

Deyá, Majorca, Spain   R. G.
1964

Mammon

Annual Oration, The London School of Economics and
Political Science, December 6, 1963

Mammon

I felt rather shaken last year when asked to deliver an annual Oration to the London School of Economics and Political Science; I concluded that the Committee must have heard of my economic and political naïveté, and of my dedication to a poetic way of thought, and wanted perhaps to hear me enlarge on the text 'If there's no money in poetry, neither is there poetry in money.'

I admit having once used this comeback on a businessman who was kindly urging me to write a best-seller rather than poems which no ordinary mortal (meaning himself) could understand. Yet poets need never have empty purses. . . . This may sound somewhat starry-eyed, like the Biblical injunction to trust in the Lord, for He will provide. . . . But since economists study the science of money, maybe they should be reminded once in a while of certain poetic and religious imponderables without which economics make no sense—or no more than do the logistical war-games, played by budding generals at Staff Colleges, which disregard such unlogistical factors in real warfare as morale, weather, accident and miracle.

Let me start with the etymology of 'money'. A word's first meaning is the usual poetic approach to its subsequent history. *Money* comes from *moneta*, a Roman surname of the goddess Juno, whose temple housed the Republican mint. *Moneta*, translated from the Greek *Mnemosyne* ('mental concentration', or 'an act of memory'), was applied to Juno in the sense that oaths to pay so many coins of approved weight and metallic fineness for land, goods or services, were sworn in her name before witnesses. Thus *moneta*, meaning 'approved coin', gradually superseded *pecunia*, or 'cattle', the old-fashioned Latin for 'money': cows having been the common standard of exchange (as they still are in parts of Africa) until abandoned because of the obvious variation in value between individual cows.

An approved coinage is the jumping-off point for the study of economic and political science; but let us go back farther in ancient history, to the idea of 'barter'; and beyond that to the idea of obligatory gift-exchanges; and beyond that, to the still purer idea of unconditional gift. What we now call 'finance' is, I hold, an intellectual perversion of what began as warm human love. To be brief: money can be redeemed from the Biblical curse put on 'filthy lucre' only by reviving in it the lost sense of a love-gift—which, of course, is most children's first introduction to money, when a kind uncle presses sixpence into their little palms. But, as I hope to show, this cannot be done except in a strictly anarchic context.

There are two primitive kinds of love: the love of a mother for her brood, and the mutual love of courting couples. Both kinds vary greatly throughout Nature, but seem strongest among birds and primates. Good mothers provide titbits for their brood even if they go hungry themselves; courting couples offer each other not only titbits, but flowers and toys—the bower-bird and the penguin are ready bird-examples—in proof of affection. A mother's impartial distribution of food starts a companionship between her children which often outlasts their need of it, so that they form packs, flocks or herds. Young monkey kinsfolk behave very well towards each other, even caring for the sick.

Primitive man, however, took co-operation a good deal further than monkeys: making, it seems, a study of insect life—as *Proverbs* enjoins the sluggard to go to the ant (and, in the original text, also to the bee), consider their ways, and be wise. Indeed, the bee was a well-known metaphor for the queen-mother of matriarchal societies. Anthropologists have noted an insectival type of communism among Australian aborigines and the Tierra del Fuegans, who do not understand private property and share all food and other booty without stint. Members of a clan are united by perfect loyalty based both on reciprocal trust and—this is important—on common mistrust, or hatred, of outsiders; even though (as anthropological field-workers agree) such loyalty is consistent with an active dislike between individual clansmen.

Elsewhere, courtship-giving becomes a metaphor for alliances between clans: each clan agreeing to supply the other with a particular product or products. The right of connubium usually seals these bargains and assures a harmonious interdependence between clans. So far, we have not left the love area, but when more gift-products get amassed than are needed, and can be safely stored, these encourage multilateral treaties. They also encourage the rise of mercantile clans who dispose of the various surpluses to outsiders. Finally, weights and measures regularize trade; and metal in ingot form is accepted as an all-purpose medium for buying and selling. Thus maternal love and courtship habits are extended, by metaphor, to loyalty inside a clan, to friendship between clans, and to good business relations between foreigners. If this were the whole history of money, how pleasant our world would be, and how simple the science of economics!

At this stage, however, a certain awkwardness arises: caused by the unnatural concept of fatherhood and the entry of male gods into religion, where hitherto the Goddess has reigned supreme. Now, the father is an unimportant figure in most natural species; often not averse to eating his own infant young, and always neglecting the survivors' education. Among birds, however, the cock is sometimes decently domesticated and helps in nest-building: the pious eider-drake, when the eider-duck has lined their nest with her breast feathers but they have been stolen to make eider-downs, will denude his own breast of its rather second-rate plumage to keep her eggs warm through an Arctic spring. Yet the cock-cuckoo—a bird-disguise which Father Zeus adopted before seducing the goddess Hera and claiming universal sovereignty— never does a claw-stroke of work.

It seems to have been late in pre-history that women's need of fertilization before child-bearing was discovered by men, who thereupon began calling themselves 'fathers'. Their jealousy of sexual rivals was sharpened by watching fights between rams and bulls for the lordship of a herd. Patriarchy is, indeed, a phenomenon associated with cattle-owning nomads who worship Bull-gods or Ram-gods. Once cattlemen claim ownership of women and their offspring, this leads to frequent fratricidal combat between would-be patriarchs, and to raids on peaceful matriarchal territory. Pastoral tribes are, as a rule, better organized for warfare than agricultural ones; and the plunder carried off tempts them to further conquests. Their disdain of the matriarchs whose land they occupy is justified by another natural analogy: woman as no more than the furrow where proud man sows his seed. In many matriarchal or matrilineal societies, a boy old enough to leave his mother's hut goes to that of her brother. In patriarchal tribes, the father claims him and he is cruelly initiated into the arts of rapine and murder. Thus fear of the father displaces love of the mother as a fundamental religious formula. The Latin word *patruus*, 'paternal uncle', always connoted severity at Rome—as it still does in patriarchal Spain, where *tio*, 'uncle', can popularly mean any harsh and difficult character; whereas *avunculus*, 'maternal uncle', carries a sense of ponderous but genuine kindness, because he need feel no legal obligation to educate his orphaned nephews.

When the ancient metaphor of maternal love that

could bind communities together by free exchange of gifts, was challenged, the contagion of patriarchal severity and greed spread everywhere. As men of the Late-Christian Era, we inherit our ambiguous attitude towards money from the Jews, whom this problem always troubled. Israel was a nation composed of two warring strains—Goddess-loving Canaanite agriculturists and God-fearing Aramean pastoralists who first subdued them under Abraham. The Aramean god El was bull-headed. However, the native cult proved too popular for suppression, even after Joshua's conquests several centuries later, and the Goddess continued in power both at Shechem and Jerusalem. Only when the Judaean monarchy neared its end did the prophets' bizarre doctrine, of a wise and loving *Father* who had deposed the lustful and irresponsible *Mother*, allow the nation to resolve its religious conflict in theory at least. (Among certain West African societies, where a son traces his descent from at least fourteen maternal ancestresses, but has no legal ties with his father, a deep and socially irrelevant affection binds these two; and it is the mother's brother, the *avunculus*, who becomes the *tio*.)

The Israelites had not been a mercantile people, except during the brief period of King Solomon's alliance with the Phoenicians; but, according to *Genesis* and the early historical books, they used gold ingots of fixed weight as the price of land. Thus Abraham paid the Hittites four Carchemish *minae* for his burial cave at Machpelah, and Jacob paid one *mina* for his plot at Shechem. If drought, pestilence or Midianite raiders forced a man to restock his farm with borrowed money, kinsmen of either party witnessed the weighing of the ingots, and such contracts were never afterwards disputed. But little love was shown in these deals. The lender took a pledge for his loan, either in land or goods, and though a limit had been set on the transfer of fields containing ancestral tombs—and therefore inalienable—a poor borrower could offer his person as a pledge and, in default of repayment, become the lender's bondman. Nevertheless, in order to keep Israel a country of small independent farms, rather than of *latifundia* worked by serf labour, the *Book of Leviticus* ruled that lands sold in this manner must revert freely to the original owner or his heirs in the 'Year of Jubilee', which came round every half-century; and that all bondmen should be released after seven years' service. The regulation did not, of course, apply to Canaanites: their perpetual serfdom being authorized by Noah's curse on his grandson Canaan, who had mischievously castrated him.

One of the last Jewish monarchs, King Josiah, published the *Book of Deuteronomy* as a merciful amendment of the earlier four books of the *Pentateuch*: Shaphan the Scribe attributing it to Moses. Lenders were now restrained from taking household necessities as pledges, or even from choosing alternative pledges, and forbidden to demand any interest on their loans; also, all debts were wiped out every seven years—these being reckoned not from the date of the contract, but from the most recent 'Year of Release'. The law assumed a degree of generosity unnatural in lenders who did not happen to be relatives, or on terms of close friendship with their borrowers. Both Josiah and Shaphan must have realized its impracticability, for Israel is enjoined: 'Beware that there be not a base thought in thine heart, saying: "The seventh year, the Year of Release, is at hand"; beware lest thine eye be evil against thy needy brother, and thou lend him naught!'

Babylonian captivity and Seleucid rule then brought the Jews into close contact with prevailing mercantile ethics, after which the richer citizens showed no inclination to make interest-free loans unless they could be certain of reimbursement. Since David (if it was David)

8

said in a Psalm that, though an old man, he had never
seen the righteous forsaken nor his children left to beg
bread, this implied that the poor were poor either as a
result of idleness or in punishment of inherited sins.

Nevertheless, shortly before Israel became absorbed by
Rome, the Messianic Pharisees reasserted the prophetic
doctrine of God's loving-kindness and man's duty to his
neighbour; and in such emphatic terms that by the reign
of the Hasmonean Queen Alexandra they had gained control of the legislature—successfully opposing the Sadducee priesthood who rejected all liberal readings of the
Mosaic Law, and interpreting the savager passages of the
first four books in humane terms. This movement indeed grew so strong that left-wing fanatics founded celi-
bate communistic settlements beside the Dead Sea—
women being naturally scornful of benevolent patriarchy
—and cut themselves off from the rest of the nation.

Other fanatics, who held that celibacy contravened
God's first Commandment, 'Increase and multiply!',
formed brotherhoods at Bethany, Emmaus, Damascus,
and elsewhere, sending out missionary groups to preach
the gospel of mercy and repentance. One of these groups
—that led by Jesus of Nazareth—attained world-wide
fame. Yet Jesus did not repudiate money as a social convenience, but paid the Sanctuary tax demanded of him,
named Judas of Cherioth the company treasurer, and
distinguished 'the Mammon of Unrighteousness' (meaning wealth won by financial craft) from 'the Mammon of
Righteousness' (meaning wealth won by honest toil or
trade). This was orthodox Pharisee dogma, based on
Scripture—namely that money in itself could be neither
good nor evil, since it had been used both for selling
Joseph into servitude, and for buying the Temple site on
Mount Zion. Jesus' reported words, 'You cannot serve
both God and Mammon', were short for 'You cannot
serve both God and the Mammon of Unrighteousness'.

He preached against the Sadducee priesthood who, though forbidden by Deuteronomic Law from distraining on a widow's garment for debt, would (in Job's words) not shrink from claiming her ox or her house, and leaving her to starve. His Sermon on the Mount, reinforced by the parable of Dives and Lazarus, showered blessings on the honest poor, and curses on the dishonest rich.

The Pharisees tried to prevent impoverished Jews from asking foreigners for loans at interest, by introducing the *prosbul*—a saving clause that enabled a creditor to demand payment of a loan at any chosen period before the next 'Year of Release'. But this clause, sponsored by Hillel, was not enough to keep the poor from becoming poorer, or the rich richer. Jesus desired to reclothe Mammon in garments of love, by contrasting the generous master, who forgave his servant a huge debt, with the same servant who seized his fellow-servant by the throat in a dispute about a far smaller sum. He also warned the disciples to think no more about tomorrow's subsistence than birds did; and answered the rich young Jew who had kept the Law meticulously and wanted some assurance of Salvation: 'One thing is wanting: sell all that thou hast and give to the poor!' An unrealistic injunction, because the earnest young man must have felt himself responsible for his dependants' livelihood, and to scatter gold at random among the city mob might have prompted crimes of violence. . . . Jesus' words should therefore be read as his ironical reproof of the young man's sanctimoniousness; and perhaps also as a plea for help—since he and his disciples were themselves deserving poor.

The economic background of their three years' missionary wanderings is seldom considered by theologians. When the ill-paid Roman legions occupied Asia Minor and Syria, rich men were bled; but poor men, skinned. Banditry, blackmail and squalor abounded. The cost of living in the Protectorate of Judaea and the small Native

State of Galilee must have been excessive. Everything was taxed separately: houses, land, fruit-trees, cattle, carts, fishing boats, market produce, salt. . . . The Romans had also imposed a poll-tax, a road-tax, a tax on exports and imports. Worse: they farmed these taxes out to financiers; who sub-leased them to contractors; who had to buy police protection. Most of the disciples were working men with families. While on the road, their annual out-of-pocket expenses—apart even from alms given to beggars—cannot have been less than the equivalent of three or four thousand pounds sterling. Surprisingly, St Luke mentions among their moneyed backers Susanna, wife of Chusa, chief finance minister to the Tetrarch of Galilee—in fact, to Herod Antipas, who had beheaded John the Baptist, and against whom Jesus himself preached!

True, this woe-to-the-rich communism, attested in the early chapters of *Acts*, soon became impractical and broke down, despite a sharp warning to the faithful when Ananias and Sapphira were struck dead in punishment for capitalistic deviation. And the Pauline Christians, having disowned the Church of Jerusalem led by St James and repudiated ritual Judaism, made light of Jesus' statement that the Mosaic Law and its Pharisaic glosses would remain in force until all prophecies were fulfilled. They held that these prophecies had been fulfilled at the Resurrection, and that the Law had no further power over believers in Jesus' godhead. Church Councils were thus free to legislate on all religious questions in His name; and to admit rich men into heaven by widening the eye of the proverbial needle. As a result, Christian monetary ethics soon corresponded closely with those of the Graeco-Roman world: the watchwords of which were *caveat emptor*, and *sine sponsione nihil*—'No loan without collateral!' Yet their Master's words—however altered or glossed by Gentile editors—remain embedded in the Gospels, and have often been taken, by Protestant and

Catholic mystics alike, as literally as he meant them.

Paul, though denouncing money-greed as the root of all evil, found himself accused of this very sin by Christian contemporaries. In the *Epistle to the Corinthians*, he justifies his use of an expense account while conveying to the Saints at Jerusalem certain alms collected for them by Asian Churches. He writes: 'I have a right to make a respectable public appearance.' These Asian Churches were not communistic; but the Jerusalem Saints still pooled their resources and spent all their time in prayer and preaching, despite the Pharisees' view that even Doctors of the Law should toil at a trade: 'Six days *shalt* thou labour!' They needed Paul's money not only to cover their own professional expenses, but to maintain their 'widows'—namely, the wives whom they had discarded on 'making themselves eunuchs for God's sake'.

Paradoxically, our international banking system was fostered by the Deuteronomic Law against interest, and by the Deuteronomic gloss on *Exodus* xxii. 25: 'Thou shalt not treat the debtor as if thou wert an usurer!'—that is, as a money-lender who demands interest. For the Jews of the Dispersal seldom broke their religious ties with Jerusalem where, when rich enough, they would annually attend the High Festivals; and, being literate members of the Synagogue, corresponded among themselves in Aramaic about business matters. Simon ben Mathias of Cyrene, say, could trust his cousin Eliezer ben Johanan of Syracuse, a God-fearing Jew, to honour his bills for any amount on an agreement reached, years before, and to ask no interest. . . . So Simon would send Eliezer a cargo of Cyrenian goods, by way of pledge for an agreed loan; and Eliezer would send Simon his Syracusan goods on the same understanding. Each made a profit on the other's pledge, but no money passed between them until accounts were settled at Jerusalem. Soon, Gentiles took advantage of this Jewish agreement, and sent goods for sale to Syracuse or Cyrene; but would, of course, pay interest on the loan at each end—Jews not being forbidden to charge a Gentile interest.

Seventeenth-century Sephardic Jews, escaping from the Inquisition to Cromwellian England, founded 'the City'. Christian bankers, in fact, could not trust one another as co-religionists to the degree that Jew could trust Jew; and, although Protestants might sing David's psalm in praise of the upright man who has refrained not only from taking bribes and bearing false witness against the guiltless, but from lending money on interest, even Christian Churches committed this sin. (The case has been obscured by use of the word 'usury', which Church-men casuistically define as *extortionate* interest: a sense missing from the Hebrew text.)

Greeks and Romans worshipped a god of Money, Hermes—also patron of Thieves and Diplomats—whom Homer celebrated for cheating the god Apollo, while still an infant, much to Father Zeus's amusement. The Christian Church frowned on this recognition of an in-born human frailty, which the Law might perhaps re-strain but could never eradicate. Yet a growing Christian disbelief in Heaven, Hell, and dogmatic theology, soon restored to Hermes, whom I prefer to call 'Mammon', his lost glory.

He is now the only god who still gives active proof of his omnipresence: changing shape continually; scattering rewards or punishments in this world rather than the problematic next; permitting his devotees to dance with the whole *corps de ballet* of Deadly Sins; encouraging a politic disguise of his worship under the mantle of Christianity; and wielding universal power—this side of the grave, at least. Jesus ironically told his hearers to make friends with the Mammon of Unrighteousness, who could offer them everlasting mansions in Heaven. . . . Yet a genuine priest of Mammon has my respect. He will be far less interested in enjoying the power that wealth gives him, than in observing its influence on trade, industry, science, art, literature, politics, entertainment, sex, religion, scholarship. . . . He will piously harden his heart while serving his god, and acquire an uncanny knowledge of this dirty world: despising all who fail to share his faith that 'there is nothing money cannot buy'; and will laugh at love as heartily as love laughs at locksmiths.

Yet his is a hard life: to disregard even minimal sums, or be awed by stupendously large ones, would be a lapse from grace. Perfect dedication to Mammon casts out all affection: the rich man bestows no costly gift on friends who once shared his poverty. And though he may maintain his parents or poor relations for fear their shabbiness may weaken his credit, or pay a prestige price for a blonde model's company, these are not weak surrenders to sentiment. Whatever luxuries he buys himself, such as works of art, country houses, or a yacht (even if he hates the sea), will be excused either as investments with untaxable capital appreciation, or as necessary proofs to his associates that he is not slipping. He cannot avoid the required year-long progress from luxury hotel to luxury hotel: must shoot grouse in Scotland; ski at Gstaad; bet at Ascot; visit his tailor in Savile Row; take his wife to the Paris Collections; attend the *feria* at Seville and the *première* of every Broadway musical— none of which events mean much to him—and spend three or four days each month in jet planes. . . . He does not, as the Banias of India, a money-lending caste, are said to do: perform his *puja* on set days before a great heap of gold coin. . . . Or does he, secretly, when he visits his private vault? Who knows?

Though aware that he can take nothing with him when death comes, he grudges large bequests to his heirs and delights meanwhile in keeping them short of cash lest they rival him in riches. Often he leaves the bulk of his property to some foundation, so that his name may endure as a successful benefactor. He judges his tips neatly, to avoid charges either of extravagance or meanness, and is seldom seen in the company of lesser financiers or common people. He may at times contribute to public charities as a means of avoiding tax; but his donation must head the list. The poor envy him; and all his companies expand and proliferate. . . .

Last year a Majorcan journalist interviewed a rich Lapp visitor to our island, and asked how many reindeer he owned. The Lapp answered, through two interpreters: 'That is a very improper question in my country: suppose I were to inquire into your bank account?'

A shrewd point. Ask an English workman: 'What's your weekly pay packet?', and the answer will seldom be grudged, since he is paid at Union rates, and his mates know it. But ask the same man: 'What money have you put by?', and he'll say: 'What business is it of yours?' Meaning: 'Don't try touching me for a fiver!' A true financier would not tell even his dying mother how much he was worth; the nurse might overhear. . . . The other day, when I put this question experimentally to a young man of independent means, he answered: 'Ask me anything else you please: my politics, my religion, my sexual preferences and technique. . . . But *that's* something I can't reveal!'

Now, he knew well enough that I wasn't going to touch him for a fiver; or advise him to give all he had to the poor; or inform on him to the Inland Revenue. . . . Only the sacredness of Mammon sealed his lips.

God's curse of mankind, 'In the sweat of thy brow shalt thou eat bread!', was taken literally by the Jews, who have never since stopped toiling with their hands or brains; and also by devout Protestants. I am conditioned that way myself, and cannot take a vacation without feelings of guilt—even at an age which would qualify me for an old-age pension, had I licked the right number of National Insurance stamps; which I haven't. Catholics, living in Catholic countries at a further remove from the Jewish ethic, find far less compulsion to work; nor, indeed, do they conscientiously feel obliged to make honest tax returns, despite Jesus' 'Render unto Caesar the things that are Caesar's!'

I asked the Israeli Income Tax chief a year or two ago: how honest were the national returns? He answered: 'Well, we still have immigrants who fail to distinguish their own government from that of the countries where they were an oppressed and unrepresented minority. So, although our returns are not yet as honest as your Protestant ones, they are far more honest than in Catholic, or Greek Orthodox, or Moslem countries.'

A Sanhedrin ruling permitted the Jews to deceive Roman-appointed tax-gatherers, who ranked with prostitutes as unfit to give sworn evidence in court. My own view of the 'Render unto Caesar' text is that Jesus must have said: '*Render not unto God that which is Caesar's!*', a reference to the blasphemous inscription on Tiberius's coinage: 'Son of the God Augustus', which banned its acceptance by the Temple Treasurers; '*Nor unto Caesar that which is God's*', namely, acknowledgment of power bestowed on him by a false god. But Jesus will at least have paid his annual poll-tax at Nazareth, since the Pharisees regarded this as a punishment ordained by God for Israel's sins, and in *Matthew* xxiii. 1 he orders his disciples to obey the Pharisees.

I never lend on interest, or even on security, to a close friend; but neither do I raise an outcry like the Moslem widow who discovered that the money she had put into a bank was yielding interest. The manager explained that interest, though forbidden by the Prophet, was inseparable from banking; and that she could always give

16

hers to the poor. 'No,' said she, 'it's not mine to dispose of. *You* give it to the poor!' 'Very well, madam! Name your charity, and send me a written authority for the transfer.' She shouted: 'How can I authorize you to dispose of what I am forbidden to acknowledge as mine?'

One can't fight Mammon. For reasons of health, I am domiciled abroad, but in theory resident here; and am taxed on my earnings at source, although disenfranchized (having had my University vote taken from me by a Labour Government and never given back by the Conservatives, as they promised). Yet I don't raise the cry 'No taxation without representation!', and continue a loyal subject of the Queen, pretending to myself that her laws are not really framed by a Cabinet led by Mammon's chief executive—the First Lord of the Treasury, whom she expects me to venerate on her account while forbidden to vote for him! And when, on legal advice, I sell my literary copyrights to a foreign company and pay a reduced tax on them—instead of the personal 7s 9d in the £, which seems inequitable since I am already taxed as a resident of Spain—the First Lord of the Treasury sends Mr Bloodsucker of the Inland Revenue to 'stop that leak' by browbeating his opposite number in the foreign country concerned, meanwhile withholding payment of my royalties at source. An odd situation. I am within my legal rights, and Mr Bloodsucker, as a civil servant, stands to gain nothing except maybe promotion by his unethical trip. And the main reason that I took legal advice was to avoid dishonesty! If taxed as a company, I need not make out an annual claim for refund on account of authorial expenses, which I can only guess at because I never keep accounts; and which Mr Bloodsucker can't check, because I live abroad; and which my income tax consultant inspires, knowing that Mr Bloodsucker takes a curious view of how writers live, and allows me necessary expenses which I do not incur, while disallowing other, more necessary ones, which I do incur. Being something of a Pharisee, I consider Mr Bloodsucker's tax a punishment inflicted on me for a failure to think poetically all the time.

Everyone, except the occasional Robinson Crusoe, or gaolbird, or insane pauper, needs money; but its distribution nowadays is eccentric, and a full purse may depend on an accident of birth, or on skill, or industry, or sleight of hand, or blind luck. In many Moslem and Catholic countries, great wealth and great poverty still co-exist, as they did at Jesus' Jerusalem. Without abundant poor, how can the faithful give abundant alms?

Ideal communism takes Aboriginal Society for its model; but all experiments in brotherly love, even when sponsored by so economically adept a philanthropist as Robert Owen, have failed unless enforced and maintained by sheer need—such as natural disasters like shipwrecks which leave survivors stranded on desert islands. Or, as in Russia after the October Revolution: a breakdown of central government. Or, as in Israel: where a constant state of emergency encouraged the growth of *kibbutzim*. Or, as in ancient Sparta: where, we are told, King Lycurgus persuaded the aristocrats to protect themselves against their Helot serfs, and against their enemies of Elis and Messene, by adopting a semi-communistic system in which, to prevent bribery, luxury and trade ties with neighbouring states, an iron coinage was struck. Brides were no longer bought, and selective breeding encouraged; all means were communal—'a Spartan diet' of bread and black broth. The Spartans admitted no foreigners to their society, with the curious exception of Alcibiades, a renegade Athenian, who in return gave them valuable strategic advice and aided the selective breeding campaign by seducing the Queen of Sparta herself. Children belonged to the State; nobody emigrated; the Spartans hated all outsiders and were hated in return. Every man knew every other man, at least by sight and reputation. And Sparta kept her nominal independence long after the Romans occupied Greece.

By the way, accounts of Spartan iron money must not be taken too literally. They come from Greek philosophers who were intent on building up in retrospect an ideal republic of dedicated citizens, and liked to forget that the regular Peloponnese currency once consisted of iron spits imported from Anatolia: iron having, by Dorian times, ousted bronze in military and agricultural use. Elsewhere, copper ingots were favoured; but when the seventh-century Lydians paid their Greek mercenaries in small silver disks (stamped with a guarantee of fineness), Athens, Thasos and other states that owned silver mines, thought this a good idea. The Spartans, who had none, imported gold and silver for personal or religious use— paying in slaves, procured by means of these same spits beaten into swords and spearheads—but found a silver currency expensive and retained the iron one. It must be remembered that iron, before the invention of Bessemer's process, did not rust so quickly. . . . Moreover, the Spartan diet of barley bread and bean soup was no better proof of austerity than a German peasant's preference for pumpernickel and beer soup; they just happened to like both.

The Soviet Russian experiment, despite an energetic propaganda against pluto-democratic bandits and Fascist beasts, has so far failed to eliminate private property. The ex-Czarist Empire proved too large and diversified a unit to accept the idea of brotherliness. Later, when all danger of foreign intervention had passed, the new proletarian dictators set out to enforce brotherliness by unbrotherly means. . . . Israel's *kibbutzim*, on the other hand, have not yet failed, partly because a sense of emergency still exists; partly, because their communism was prompted by so genuine a sense of brotherhood and sisterhood that most old members would be ashamed to quit. Yet the *kibbutzim* have not kept pace with the rise in population, and some are now reduced to hiring immigrant labour.

Of the two power-blocs disputing for world sovereignty, one is controlled by Mammon-lovers; one by Mammon-fearers. Although the Mammon-fearers preach ideal communism, under which everyone labours for the nation's good, they enforce it not only by honours and rewards for honest work that should be its own reward, but by imprisonment and even capital punishment for evasion of honest work. And they strengthen their cause by the same psychological means that disgraced the mediaeval Church, and Czarism.

As for Mammon-lovers, they have long been busily securing raw materials at bargain prices, capturing world trade by the sale of manufactured goods at sharp prices, and doing all they can to ingratiate themselves with the governments of underdeveloped countries. Their aim is to confer on the poor, benighted foreigner a richer and more civilized way of life. . . . Yet many warm-hearted Americans travelling abroad are shocked to find that a prodigal Foreign Aid programme has not made them any more loved than their British predecessors—whom they have out-bought and out-sold by a more efficient cult of Mammon—indeed, on the whole, rather less.

Not only is it certain that money cannot buy love; but —as the millionaire play-boy once told a designing starlet—'Love cannot buy money.'

Since international capitalism goes under democratic disguise and has not so far taken over more than a small part of the civilized world (by controlling industry, science, education, entertainment), a freedom-loving poet may still escape to some region where he can disregard politics, think, do and say what he pleases, and print his own books without an official *imprimatur*. A dictatorship of the proletariat rules out such freedoms; whereas capitalism, by its very inefficiency in standardizing appetites and habits, has become a shield for people who neither love nor fear money, and cannot be much interested in the rules that govern its distribution, unless trade cycles temporarily keep them short of food.

Most Englishmen will entertain a friend or even a stranger, at considerable cost; yet they baulk at offering a gift of money—except to children, professional beggars, or organized charity: gifts must always be disguised as loans. Moreover, blasphemy against Mammon is far more dangerous nowadays than blasphemy against God. The old atheistic trick of taking out a watch and giving God two minutes to strike one dead—Mussolini used to do that as a young man; but God's mills grind slowly—is less shocking than to tear up a five-pound note and let the wind carry away its pieces. . . .

I know few Englishmen capable of such an act, even though the paper has no intrinsic value and its destruction can be praised as a patriotic lowering of the national debt. I very much doubt whether I could do it myself; but then I have a Protestant conditioning which, though I am no longer a believer, still prevents me, for instance, from laying a book on top of a Bible, even a Biblical Concordance; or from throwing away a crust of bread without making the sign of the cross on it. . . . My rationalization of such piety towards a Bank of England note would be: 'Anyone watching would feel enraged that I had not let it blow, untorn, down the street: for himself, or some other lucky fellow, to pocket quietly. . . .' But suppose I destroyed it in private? Would I not suffer feelings of guilt towards my poorer friends who might have made good use of it?

A holiday incident from my North Welsh childhood comes to mind. We had bought teas at a lake-side farm; afterwards I went to play in the farmyard. When a wagonette drove up with more visitors, I ran to open the gate. Someone tossed me a sixpence, and though I did not throw it back, the idea that my disinterested courtesy had been mistaken for money-making shocked me. . . . My male ancestors had always been professional men—doctors, scholars, clergy and civil servants—and always intermarried with their own kind. At home, we despised trade of any sort, and to this patrician prejudice was added a secretive hardness about money—very much like the family attitude towards sex—meant to rob its possession or use of all joy. I was stinted of pocket money as a child, and still occasionally dream of picking up pennies by the hatful in a park; so that finding sixpence on a pavement now makes me feel infinitely richer than any royalty cheque.

Mammon is a merciless god and a cruel master; yet I have found him a good domestic servant if treated firmly and generously and never spied upon. If ever I get into serious trouble, he has always responded to my considera-tion for his feelings by coming at once to my rescue: for instance on Christmas Day, 1924, when I was living in an Oxfordshire cottage with my wife and three children, on a small wound pension, occasional book reviews, and the sale of my library. I had twenty-five shillings in my pocket, and none in the bank, but I gave five shillings as a Christmas box to Mr Launchbury the postman who brought me a batch of Christmas cards and a registered letter. 'I hope it's a hundred pounds, sir,' he said smiling, as I signed for the letter, 'and a merry Christmas to you!' It *was* a hundred-pound note, sent me by a man whom I had met, casually, once or twice: William Kiddier, a brush manufacturer from Nottingham. He wrote: 'I have had a good year, I like your poems, and I hear you are in difficulties. Please show your friendship by accepting this. And a merry Christmas to you.' Kiddier's gift saved the situation, and although (until about six years ago) I never had saved enough to allow for more than six months' sub-sistence, Mammon never failed me, because (as my mother would have said) I 'put him upon his good behaviour . . .' Chief among Mammon's agents was T. E. Lawrence who believed, as I did, that, after one's own reasonable necessities and obligations had been taken care of, money should be at the disposal of one's friends.

A common fallacy held by idealist philosophers, religious fanatics and liberal politicians is that everyone can love everyone else. Sometimes an enforced neighbourliness, especially in wartime, will extend the circle of love to include people with whom as a rule one has nothing in common; but once the danger has passed it soon shrinks again to a few shining names. I dislike organized charities. Too high a percentage of what is collected goes to pay the organizers; nor can I feel genuine love for the nameless beneficiaries, or expect any from them. . . . The hungry children of Central Europe, on whose account, in 1920, I sold my gold watch and a few wedding presents, had grown into brawny Nazis by the nineteen-forties and were taking their revenge on me and my family for Lloyd George's and Clemenceau's mercilessness.

There is no more ironical story in the whole Bible than Jesus' praise of the poor widow who gave her last two mites to the Temple Treasury. Two days later, Judas's thirty pieces of silver came out of this very collection, most of which went to support a priesthood whom Jesus had just condemned as traitors; while the rest paid for further barbaric embellishment of a Temple whose imminent destruction he had already prophesied. . . .

I carry no life assurance—not only because the real value of money has been falling for the last fifty years, so that one gets back far less than one puts in—but because it shows a lack of trust in my servant Mammon. Mammon has treated me honestly, despite my ambiguous dealings with Mr Bloodsucker, and never heaped my lap with such superfluity of riches that I felt tempted to stop working even one day in seven, or to take vacations. I do not (as I say) keep accounts, leaving that to my bank and literary agents; so long as I know roughly what reserves I have, personal accounts are a waste of time and would hamper my spending and giving. William Kiddier's hundred pounds has never been out of my mind: he honoured me by trusting that I would accept it without embarrassment, as he himself would have done had our positions been reversed. Nor can I forget how T. E. Lawrence, when I was lured into an unlucky trading venture, sent me four chapters of his *Seven Pillars of Wisdom* to sell to an American magazine, explaining that honour would not let him touch any money the book might make—and he never did—but that these two hundred pounds should put me straight.

I would be the last to force on any one of you a view of money that runs counter to his upbringing. I admit my individual disregard of common economic practice; and spend money only where my heart lies or need calls. Mammon will always honour the calm conviction of financial stability which is called 'credit', and appear when called.

I never read economic text-books, but the general trend seems clear enough. There will always be more money tomorrow than yesterday, and it will always be worth less; food will become progressively more insipid; goods progressively more expendable, which means less lovable. All surviving hand-made objects of merit will be collected in museums (and thus withdrawn from circulation). Mammon's metallic coinage will cease, and so will poets; and, on attaining complete automation—the economist's *ne plus ultra*—mankind, then crowded on the earth's surface, at least a hundred souls per acre (at different levels under and above ground, that is), will be faced with the fearful problem of how to while away its leisure time except in perfect sameness of experience, and look wistfully back at these hectic days of disorganized unbrotherliness. Unless, of course, a philanthropic virus intervenes and reduces the bemused survivors to a simpler economy.

Nine Hundred Iron Chariots

Arthur Dehon Little Memorial Lecture, Massachusetts
Institute of Technology, Boston, May 14, 1963

Nine Hundred Iron Chariots

Since my election to the venerable Oxford Chair of Poetry, I have often been mistaken for a respectable public figure, and four American universities have recently wanted to make me their guest poet. I declined politely. Though my Oxford obligations are no great burden, and can be annually settled in two months or less, I grudge every hour spent away from my home among the rocks and olives of Majorca, except on important business. Yet among my latest preoccupations has been a wish to discover the mystique behind modern science: so, on being invited to spend two weeks on the M.I.T. campus as the Arthur D. Little Lecturer, I thought: 'This is it! Nowhere in the world can a more massive concentration of scientific thought be found than at M.I.T. Let me pretend for once that I am a respectable public figure, and investigate.'

I understand that back in the dark days of this Institute many senior technologists had been reluctant to admit the Humanities as a serious element in M.I.T.; and I quite see their point. It must have seemed a dangerous concession to an unworthily haphazard way of thinking: how could any Humanity side compare in its dedicated organization of purpose with the Scientific side? Last June I heard the American Secretary of State, Dean Rusk, make an off-the-record after-dinner speech at St John's College, Oxford—of which we both are members—to the effect that at no major American university do the Humanities keep abreast in thought with Science.

M.I.T. is different—I have visited a dozen or more American universities in the last few years and I recognize this difference. It did something altogether new early in the present century, when a close integration was made between the two sides by a rule that no student could become a technologist without spending a large part of his time at work among the humanists and *vice versa*. M.I.T. has a strong social conscience, as was borne in upon me last week when I was allowed to attend a session of the Zacharias Committee which plans new educational skills. But though there are at least three professors here who can think in poetic terms, the Humanities are still no more than the steadying tail of the technological kite now being carried up far out of sight on an endless weightless irrefragable string.

Your most advanced technologists remind me of a school picnic, when an adventurous young gang runs off through the woods, blazing no trail, taking with them all the Coca-Cola, and thoughtlessly leaving their friends miles behind to lug along the baskets of beef-sandwiches, cookies and blueberry pie. Yes, you want to explore; and I won't pretend that love of exploration has not been one of my own main motive forces. But the very first rule for explorers should be: keep touch with slower members of the group—at any rate with those in charge of the picnic basket!

It is politely assumed here that scientists have souls as well as minds. A non-denominational chapel is available for your convenience, and you are invited to meditate there peacefully in the intervals between religious services. A beautifully technological derrick is provided to hoist the necessary religious symbol into a commanding position. The aisles are tranquil enough, and certainly not over-crowded; but what modern scientist has ever learned the technique of meditation? Nor are any non-denominational instructions provided. With all respect to the Institute's authorities, squash-racket courts might have been more acceptable—I know no better game for healthy exercise in a limited space. Meditation, if one is faced with a scientific problem that needs no technical apparatus, requires an unfurnished, sound-proof, preferably white-washed cell. But if the scientist decides to meditate on spiritual problems (though, scientifically speaking, this would be playing hookey) no chapel, however undenomi-national, can compare with a wood—an honest-to-God self-sown wood of mixed trees, not a well-spaced Douglas fir plantation laid out by the forestry department.

Tree-magic, according to Oriental and Occidental mys-tics alike, favours meditation. But 'magic' is a poetic, not a scientific, term; modern science was established to guard rational man against a superstitious acceptance of magic and old wives' tales. And if, using technological terms, I suggest that in an anthropo-dendroid symbiosis certain tree-radiations beneficially affect man's meditative facul-ties, you must suspend judgment on my theory until it has been subjected to controlled experiment involving num-erous imponderables. You will have first to decide in what precise region of the brain these peculiar faculties operate, and then you will have to choose a theme for simultaneous meditation by a number of human controls: thus circum-scribing or negating the magic.

Here is a simple proposition. The poet and the scientist, who evidently stand at opposite extremes of contemporary thought, are both men. Sometimes, even, they are born in the same bed, eat at the same table, attend the same school, sing in the same choir. . . . But soon they grow mentally alienated; never later, in my experience, than the age of twelve. I don't think we need disagree on what we mean by 'scientists' or what we mean by 'poets'. Granted, there are casual labourers, clerks and petty officials by the hun-dred thousand listed on the pay-roll of Science, who might just as well be hewing coal, selling lingerie, or supervising children's playgrounds. Granted, also, countless volumes of new verse are published every year, though only two or three have the root of poetry in them. Let us therefore concentrate on the dedicated scientist and the dedicated poet, whose work seems to themselves the main justification for their existence, and who have earned the grudging respect of their fellows by the way they set about it.

The difference is, roughly, that the scientist concentrates on analysis and classification of external fact even if fact be beautifully disguised as mathematic relation; whereas the poet concentrates on discovery of internal truth. To a poet, analysis and factual classification are a reputable pursuit only so long as they serve a natural human need—which they often do in medicine, geology, or botany; not when they become obsessive and inhuman. I applaud, for instance, Dr Norbert Wiener's brilliant use of severed nerve-ends to give a man whose leg has been amputated control of an artificial one. To a scientist, 'internal truth' makes no sense because it defies analysis: that is to say, no factual question on the subject of internal truth, requiring a factual answer, or even a hypothetical question requiring a hypothetical answer, can be fed even to an electronic computer. So when the poet insists on internal truth, the scientist must rebuff him with: 'This is, I fear, a concept to discuss with a theologian or metaphysician.' Scientific treatises on such subjects as the comparative density of astral bodies, or the microscopic analysis of a cheese-mite's digestive system, are of small interest to a poet, who foresees no immediate contact with either phenomenon; and the scientist himself is interested in them only as pieces missing from a very small corner of the trillion-dollar jigsaw puzzle that will never, by definition, be completed. Poetry means little to a scientist, because the receiving apparatus of his brain is no longer attuned, if it ever was, to the emotional wave-length on which poems are carried; indeed, a fundamental laboratory rule forbids the admittance of emotion into any experiment, lest it should misinterpret fact. Yet scientists will agree, if pressed, that a marked physical effect may be produced on readers by certain rhythmic arrangements of words, though one neither quantitatively nor qualitatively predictable even in readers of uniform age and background. Too many imponderables again.

These contrastive preoccupations—the scientist's with fact, and the poet's with truth—give them a different attitude to environment. The scientist prefers what is neat, organized, and stable; the poet, what is unique and imponderable. Young scientists can readily be recruited and trained with the help of public money. I forget the name of the Ionian Greek meteorologist who first suggested the financial exploitation of science by predicting a severe winter (which would naturally cause a bumper olive crop, after several poor ones) and then buying up the olive presses in proof of his conviction. Politicians and industrialists have never forgotten this lesson. They house technologists like silkworms in perforated cigar boxes, supply fresh mulberry leaves once a week, and leave them to spin silk. The dependence of M.I.T. on the automobile industry is well known and acknowledged. Poets keep themselves, and are virtually unemployable.

Nowadays, the richer a nation grows, the greater its demand on scientists for new industrial techniques, means of communication and transport, armaments. These require experimental apparatus far beyond the individual's purse: hence the ever-expanding universities and technological institutes. A scientist no longer works at home; even if he can keep abreast of the copious multi-lingual literature which concerns his special field, he must join a university or technological institute. There he must conform to a particular way of life, which will accentuate his purely scientific outlook. The poet avoids conformity. If he has solved the problem of how to support himself outside academic, governmental or commercial institutions, he makes his home either in real country, or in the asphalt jungle of a city's warehouse district where almost anything may happen and where almost nothing repeats itself.

To the scientist, all phenomena are ideally of equal interest. Yet he recognizes that the ratiocinatory, electrically-propelled organism which he calls 'ME'—*cogito, ergo sum*—has to be handled with care. In short, he must eat, drink, sleep, take regular exercise, not stint his sexual appetite, allow himself a modicum of social intercourse and an occasional vacation; but he must subordinate these extra-curricular activities—even chess and classical music —to his obsession for classifying facts and, when he graduates from facts, to his curiosity about pure physics. So he is, in general, healthy, sober, co-operative, reliable, industrious; though with little perception of the magical, and emotionally underdeveloped.

Here, for the record, let me distinguish between magic and sorcery. Sorcery is an attempt to formalize magic and use it for personal ends against whoever lacks the self-confidence to combat the attack. The ideal scientist, of course, is proof against sorcerers, since he does not recognize magic and has, besides, studied the technique of hypnosis, which is the main weapon of sorcerers. His modest, almost monastic, self-sufficiency served him well in the palmy days of classical science, when all observable phenomena conformed closely enough to Nature's Iron Laws, and when the answers supplied by the abacus made immediate sense. Yet these Laws now show an increasingly limited relevance to certain new-found aspects of the microcosm and macrocosm; and some answers given by the latest computers to the latest questions make merely cosmic sense—that is to say, they can no longer be imaginatively grasped by the human brain in any predictable stage of development, and refer to processes, not to phenomena.

I need not labour this very serious point. That you have broken through to a region of non-sense—whether you spell it with a hyphen or without, does not make much odds in the long run—is an open secret. The adventurous gang who ran off into the woods, grabbing the Coca-Cola and leaving behind the beef-sandwiches, cookies and blue-berry pie, are not Indians, or even boy scouts; and when they see their compass needle whirling madly around, wonder what on earth to do next. But they share out the Coca-Cola, sing a song of spacemanship to restore their courage, and push on, farther and farther, through virgin timber, in the general direction of Labrador, or the Northwest Territory, where the nightmarish Wendigo of madness hunts its prey.

They are not likely to meet a poet in those wilds; and even if they do, the sole exchange of greetings can be a polite 'Hi!' Yet if a stray anthropologist happens to cross their path, they would be wise to consult him. Anthropo-logists are a connecting link between poets and scientists; though their field-work among primitive peoples has often made them forget the language of science. To understand how savages think and act, the thesis that there are such things as magic, oracular prophecy and divine possession has to be conceded. But soon these field-workers stop putting quotation marks around these phenomena when taking notes; and once they have joined in the ceremonial rites, so as to get a subjective picture of them, they are *cotched*. I know two women anthropolo-gists who, having been enstooled as queen-mothers of different tribes in West Africa, are now no more scientists than I am. Each talks of 'my people' with the mystical seriousness that, for example, enhanced two very run-of-the-mill English naval officers, George V and George VI —neither of them born heir to the throne—into real kings by the Grace of God. Yes, I know, the British Constitution limits sovereignty to what appears a mere parade of outworn magnificence; but the less executive power a sovereign has, the stronger the magic—especially with a queen. (If Queen Victoria had been reigning in 1776, instead of her mad grandfather. . . . But neither you nor I can afford to speculate on historical hypotheses.)

Well, now that electronic computers have passed the limits of the brain's imaginative grasp, physicists should consult an anthropologist who still speaks their own scientific language, and let themselves be reassured that vast tracts of human thought remain to be explored, which the computer knows nothing of and which call for no complex apparatus.

Here, at the risk of seeming to bite the hand that has so generously fed and cosseted me—I must say that I have never, repeat never, been so welcomed by any university on either side of the Atlantic—let me make a criticism. When the question came up in the Zacharias Committee, 'Should philosophy continue to be taught here as a special subject?' and I was invited to answer, I said: 'For me, philosophy is a peculiar disease of thought most readily understandable by reference to the Athenian environment where it first hardened: in an atmosphere of more or less uninhibited thought, slave labour, the rich Laurion silver mines, a powerful fleet, the subjection of women, ideal pederasty. Philosophy is a subject for anthropologists. So also are, for example, such strange phenomena as the self-perpetuating Freudian priesthood disguised as a scientific college; the equally unscientific and self-perpetuating Communist priesthood; non-figurative art; and philately. With a simple anthropological background, students should be able to figure these phenomena out for themselves without spending much time in their detailed study.' To provide an anthropological department at M.I.T. would cost three million dollars, or so I was told. So what? Three million bucks are mere chicken feed.

A study of anthropology would remind the student that civilization has been developing at different speeds in different parts of the world for several thousand years. The more successful nations, judged in terms of military strength, communications, productivity and trade, do not govern all the less successful ones; yet they do force them to imitate the Western way of life. Although originally the avowed aim was to evangelize all benighted heathen —the Spaniards and Portuguese began this; the English, Dutch and French followed—no historian will challenge the Oriental saying: 'First Bible; then enamel basin; then bayonet.'

After the bayonet came roads, railways, factories, hospitals, famine relief, striped trousers and bowler hats, bureaucrats, automobiles, parliamentary voting, scientific institutions. . . . The few primitive areas left in Africa, New Guinea and Oceania, have shrunk to pocket-handkerchief size. Another twenty years, and they will have faded away altogether. Of course, the bayonet is now out-of-date, replaced by the submachine-gun; so is the enamel basin, replaced by a plastic bowl; and so, with all respect, is the Bible. Big business, which controls all modern states, has trodden in the missionary's footsteps and used the Judaeo-Christian ethic, based squarely on the Bible, in support of its policies. Yet no scientist, however specialized his field, can factually accept even the *Book of Genesis*; and what the scientist thinks today, everyone else will think the day after tomorrow.

I should like you to feel nostalgic about the picnic basket that got left behind; though I have described its contents in New England terms—which differ somewhat from Mark Twain's Missouri ones. He wrote in his *Autobiography*:

It was a heavenly place for a boy, that farm of my uncle John's. The house was a double log one, with a spacious floor (roofed in) connecting it with the kitchen. In the summer the table was set in the middle of that shady and breezy floor, and the sumptuous meals—well, it makes me cry to think of them! Fried chicken, roast pig; wild and tame turkeys, ducks and

geese; venison just killed; squirrels, rabbits, pheasants, par-
tridges, prairie-chickens; biscuits, hot batter cakes, hot buck-
wheat cakes, hot 'wheat bread', hot rolls, hot corn pone; fresh
corn boiled on the ear, succotash, butter-beans, string-beans,
tomatoes, peas, Irish potatoes, sweet potatoes; buttermilk,
sweet milk, 'clabber'; watermelons, musk-melons, canta-
loupes—all fresh from the garden; apple pie, peach pie, pump-
kin pie, apple dumplings, peach cobbler—I can't remember
the rest. The way that the things were cooked was perhaps the
main splendour—particularly a certain few of the dishes. For
instance, the corn bread, the hot biscuits and wheat bread and
the fried chicken. These things have never been properly
cooked in the North. . . .

That really was food! In our Majorcan village, we still
eat real food; and in the back streets of Palma de Mallorca,
our provincial capital, the habit lingers obstinately. But
the thousand or more tourist hotels, residences, pensions
and restaurants that now dominate our economy, have
switched to the modern cuisine insisted upon by their
guests. Now, though I don't want to be personal or to
denigrate American food, which is at least as good as
what I get in England, can you imagine any modern
Mark Twain, grown to manhood, celebrating the good-
ness of today's home cooking—which for all but those in
the top income brackets means battery broilers, battery
eggs, the latest battery veal, vegetables grown in chemi-
cally-manured soil and consigned to cans or the deep-
freeze, processed meat in cans, tasteless cottony white
bread, processed cereals, sterilized milk, canned blueberry
pie, canned crêpes suzette, even canned rice pudding?
Well, if you can't imagine, here is a bit of science fiction
to help. . . . Your children, in their old age—unless they
have somehow controlled what are called 'the social con-
sequences of science'—will be living on protein steaks
worked up from petroleum or plancton but synthetically
flavoured and handsomely technicoloured, and on hydro-

ponically raised vegetables, all sent thermo-sealed down the conveyor-belts of the Federal Foodstuff Factory. *These* will then be the good old days of home cooking!

A young farmer from the Channel Islands visited me not long ago; he raises early potatoes and tomatoes for the London market. I asked whether he still fertilized his crops with seaweed, as his father had done. He laughed unpleasantly. 'What? And put at least another penny a pound on the wholesale price? No, chum, I don't! If I did, I couldn't be here on holiday.'

'Surely,' I said, 'seaweed makes a lot of difference to the taste?'

'Maybe it does; but I'm not selling to choosey individuals like you. I'm selling to the big dealers. They care only for size and condition; don't give a damn for taste. I do use seaweed, though, for my early daffodils. Gives them a deeper colour, and I get a bob a hundred more. But whether they *taste* better, I wouldn't know.'

Now, I'm not saddling you technologists with all the shortcomings of the businessman whose pockets you have filled by showing how to process foodstuffs. These innovations have, I know, saved housewives an excessive deal of labour, and set them free, if they wish, to improve their minds by reading or watching television, or to go out and take jobs. But the result of our highly artificial urban life is that you forget how delicious old-fashioned cookery can be, or at least you resign yourselves to the new diet. Worse, no sound medical evidence has yet been adduced to show that this new rationalized cuisine does the eater any harm, so long as vitamin deficiencies are corrected and the diet balanced. Zest comes from the sauce bottle.

Science fights a little shy of taste as a phenomenon impossible to measure or describe, since different human subjects will react differently to experimental tests; nor can it be connected with the economy of digestion since, for example, the most poisonous of all mushrooms, the *amanita phalloides*, tastes most delicious—famous last words!—and insipid food nourishes no worse than the savoury. Scientists, however, find taste difficult to distinguish from smell—though gorse blossom smells as coconut tastes, whereas coconuts do not smell as gorse blossom tastes—to which they willingly concede nutritive value since, in times of famine, children have been kept alive by being laid in the street above the vent of a baker's shop. . . .

However, I use *taste* here as a metaphor for taste in the wider sense, which is one way of establishing internal truth. And I don't mean 'good taste', as sold in bulk by fashion magazines to the middle income group: good taste, the commodity which falls a little below the daringly advanced or the authenticated antique, but which is carefully distinguished from the popular. I mean personal taste, intuitive certitude in the way one dresses, reads, furnishes a room, chooses friends, and treats music. A sudden loss of internal truth, by the acceptance of a false situation, can always be noted in the loss of hitherto unerring personal taste.

I have been told that a finished product of M.I.T. can follow literary and historical and artistic discussions far better at least than the humanists of other universities can follow the scientific way of thought. No doubt; but you must understand that taste does not enter into these discussions. The teaching of the Humanities, however well taught, since supported by the same funds that support you, is based on at least semi-scientific principles: masterpieces of literature, art, and criticism being explained deterministically and classified in terms of technical accomplishment. Taste is excluded from the curriculum. A sensitive student must read numerous works as offensive to his taste as they are irrelevant to his education. The personally unique is necessarily neglected by the text-books, and so is everything that justifies its appearance.

Let me, with apparent ingratitude, parenthetically venture a further criticism of M.I.T. by calling attention to the weakest link in the technologico-humanitarian symbiosis. The brain is here regarded as an electrical apparatus. Fair enough. Complex communication between brain and brain is first achieved by some obscure sort of telepathy, then by language, finally by written words. To achieve perfect communication the writer must take cognizance of the receptive system in the reader's brain and send it messages free from fading, atmospheric crackling, stridency and short circuits, so that the semantic flow is not interrupted at any point. The scientific study of English in this sense has never been attempted at M.I.T., and among the worst offenders against clarity of communication are the leading authorities on the functions of the brain. Myself I have for some years now written all my prose at least six times over, with the help of a secretary whom I have trained to catch faults that miss my own eye, reducing each message to its clearest and simplest form, and preventing the unintended and irrelevant mating of words which have a similarity in sound, or phrases which have a similarity of rhythm; such matings are as a rule not consciously noted by the eye, but they distract the brain. And the memory length of words used in a narrative passage is far greater than the writer is aware. This is a highly specialized study, but I guarantee to prove the use of this skill, without the least contradiction, to any specialist in semantics who is also a specialist in brain signals.

On every academic roll, dullards and phoneys necessarily outnumber the real writers, artists and thinkers. In science, of course, phoneys are soon detected; unless, as happens in a few unenlightened universities, department heads claim credit for original work done by their assistants. And even these cases fall short of complete phoniness, since the fabric of science is, in theory, anonymous;

and the department-head may himself have been robbed of credit for original work by his predecessor. Moreover, what does 'original' mean? Often a discovery of great moment results from random experiment, and its implications are grasped with no expense of mental effort. That is not original work; but more like being bequeathed money by a great-aunt whom you never met.

True originality implies a leap taken by the mind across a dark gulf of nothingness into new regions of scientific thought, and the establishing of a bridgehead on the far side to help routine scientists across. Eratosthenes, Newton, Einstein, Planck, Bohr: you know their names and achievements better than I do. But men of this calibre have always been hopelessly outnumbered by the routineers of science, from whom original work is not expected. Nor, during the long, flat period of the eighteenth century, was it required of the poetic routineer; he earned far greater respect for his servile imitations of the classics than for felicitous new verbal coinages. Nowadays, however, poetic originality is insisted upon, and the routineers must pretend to possess it, by embellishing their poems with rhetorical tropes borrowed from abstractionism, psycho-analysis, and undigested foreign literature.

The original scientist may find some analogy between his experiences and a poet's. Let me present the case in technological terms. Poetry proper is written mainly by men between fifteen and twenty-seven years old— though cases are known of people writing poems at an advanced age. . . . (Women's poetry belongs to a different study altogether, no less rewarding.) The poet is, on the whole, anti-authoritarian, agoraphobic and intuitive rather than intellectual; but his judgments are coherent. Symptoms of the trance in which poetic composition occurs differ greatly from those of an induced mediumistic trance; though both seem directed by an external power.

In a poetic trance, which happens no more predictably than a migraine or an epileptic fit, this power is traditionally identified with the ancient Muse-goddess. All poems, it seems, grow from a small verbal nucleus gradually assuming an individual rhythm and verse form. The writing is not 'automatic', as in a mediumistic trance when the pen travels without pause over the paper, but is broken by frequent critical amendments and excisions. And though the result of subsequently reading a poem through may be surprise at the unifying of elements drawn from so many different levels of consciousness, this surprise will be qualified by dissatisfaction with some lines. Objective recognition of the poem as an entity should then induce a lighter trance, during which the poet realizes more fully the implications of his lines, and sharpens them. The final version (granted the truthfulness of its original draft, and the integrity of any secondary elaboration) will hypnotize readers who are faced by similar problems into sharing the poet's emotional experience.

I left out an element from my proposition about scientists and poets standing at opposite extremes of contemporary thought: namely, that mankind is composed of men and women; and that woman's thought now oscillates between two extremes—quasi-male and authentic female. Authentic female thought, though a matter of indifference to scientists, is of supreme importance to poets. . . . In 1960, when I was flying from London to Geneva on a twin-engined plane, my eight-year-old son stood up, looked out of the windows, and asked: 'Father, why is there only one propeller going round?' The Swiss air-hostess stood aghast and dropped her tray. The pilot, also noticing the anomaly, flew us back to London. Let me ask the same question about science: 'Why is there only one propeller going round?'

Almost every poet has a personal Muse, a relationship

first introduced into Europe from Sufi sources in Persia and Arabia during the early Middle Ages. She embodies for him the concept of primitive magic; and even if an occasional poet divines the Muse's existence from other poetic work and from natural surroundings traditionally associated with her immanence—such as mountains, woods and seas—his sense of possession by her is real enough. Once the Muse takes individual form, she remains absolutely free and in control of the situation. The poet-Muse relationship can never be a domestic one, nor need it be sexually consummated; since, despite all the symptoms of romantic love, it belongs to another order of experience—which, for want of a better term, we must call 'spiritual' and which is usually characterized by remarkable telescopings of space and time and by cosmic coincidences. These coincidences are not wondered at because, though rationally inexplicable, they have clearly been created by the power of thought. To enlarge on such phenomena would lead me into tedious anecdote— of the sort I recorded some eight years ago in a true story, called *The Whittaker Negroes*, and again in my account of how I wrote *The White Goddess*.

I have discussed this way of thought, which ties time into knots, with Dr Martin Deutsch, one of the scientists here whom I most wanted to meet; and he accepts it as what he calls 'structural thought', which cannot be criticized or negatived by rationalists since each occurrence is by definition unique. He told me frankly, nevertheless, that if any of his students thought in that style he would have to shake the poor fellow's hand sincerely and send him away. But this is the way poets work.

Professor Whitehead warned you when he gave his famous Harvard address of 1925:

We are now so used to the materialistic way of looking at things, which has been rooted in our literature by the genius

44

of the seventeenth century, that it is with some difficulty that we understand the possibility of another mode of approach to the problem of Nature. In the eighteenth century, the mechanical explanation of all the processes of Nature—which, to these men of science, was a dull affair, soundless, scentless, colourless—finally hardened in a dogma of science.

Dr J. P. Hodin points out that Goethe had anticipated Whitehead by over one hundred years. Goethe wrote:

Both microscopes and telescopes shift man's real standpoint. The increase in mechanization frightens me. Nobody knows himself now, nobody understands the element in which he lives and moves. Railways, express-mails, steam-ships, and every possible facility for communication are what the civilized world is after. . . . Man is not born to solve the riddles of the universe, but to keep within the limits of the comprehensible.

Goethe advised a return to God and Nature's Iron Laws, which he argued, were always right. But are they? Surely the scientist is also one of God's creatures? My old nurse used to say: 'If God had meant us to fly, He would have given us wings.' God had already done worse, or better, by letting us develop the internal combustion engine and furnish it with a glider and a joy-stick. And Nature, as Tennyson noted, is 'red in tooth and claw'. Besides, at this stage one can't turn Luddite and smash the machines; nor has the average British and American citizen any passionate complaint against our modern way of life. When he tries a holiday in some underdeveloped country, boldly renting a house in what seem ideal surroundings, he finds himself overwhelmed by the primitive problems of light, fuel, plumbing, transport, communication, entertainment. And the food has too emphatic a taste. . . .

Yet to allow a complete break with history by the universal extension of modern living would be most foolish.

I deplore the use made of institutional religion—once a bulwark against the advance of materialistic philosophy —to buttress the materialistic system; but I should equally dislike seeing it suppressed in a rationalist campaign for Godlessness. I deplore, also, the engulfing of primitive, magic-making societies by the steel jaws of modernism. What I should like to see is cultural reserves, protected from all outside influence, even from anthropological study—the natives being left enough fertile land and animal life to give them a decent chance of survival. If our own highly artificial culture blows up, only such reserves can preserve humanity. Yet, unless this scheme were sponsored by leading scientists of all nationalities, no politician would agree to protect any society, however small and remote, against infiltration by tourists or traders.

It is most improbable that a world congress of scientists —though alone of all professional men, except perhaps soldiers, they understand each other perfectly—could ever decide what limits to set on new experiment and on the exploitation of discoveries already made. And I am not singling out nuclear experiment and the missile craze which, to me, seem relatively unimportant compared with the upset of Nature's balance by irresponsible use of chemicals; the weakening, by labour-saving devices, of man's power to cope with moral or physical problems; the dulling of his imagination by commercialized art, literature, drama and music; the speed-up of communications which makes privacy almost unattainable; and the standardizing of all objects in domestic and public service. No attempt to halt progress (or regress) has ever succeeded.

When it comes to communications, scientists are naturally far more interested in the means of conveying messages than in the messages themselves, even if spectacularly bounced off the moon or exchanged between astronauts; and it is here that the width of the gap separating science from the humanities shows most comically. . . . As for the standardizing of industrial goods: I admit it has its advantages, such as a reduction of the working week by nearly a half, in an era when progressively fewer people take any pride in their work; but its disadvantages must not be forgotten. The human eye easily tires of machine-drawn straight lines and geometrical curves and of identical sets of objects, and can overcome fatigue reactions caused in this way only by ceasing to value singularity.

Goethe was right to emphasize the value of intuition and of contemplating, rather than categorizing, trees, flowers and natural objects. Unfortunately, he claimed to be following the bright beam that joined him to God; I say 'unfortunately' because this God was a Brocken Spectre of his own male self. The German language does not allow for a female Wisdom, any more than it allows for a female Moon; and in my view the political and social confusion of these last 3,000 years has been entirely due to man's revolt against woman as a priestess of natural magic, and his defeat of her wisdom by the use of intellect. He has given her the choice of becoming either a housewife, a play-thing, or a careerist. If a careerist, she remains 'auxiliary male personnel' until she manages to get control at the office; whereupon she turns honorary patriarch, and thinks along male lines. There are even a few women scientists.

I should not be speaking in this outrageous manner, unless I countered on finding among you some, at least, who have given thought to these matters. Not merely to the case of institutional religion which many men here, though scientists, schizophrenetically accept for the sake of their families. Not merely to the problem of how to keep your discoveries from being exploited in a way that robs life of its natural savour—having, as it were, chartered your ship for a voyage not your own. Not merely to the problem of how to retain particular awareness of particular living things, though you must also deal in generalities and analytical abstraction. But to the problem of what sustains you here—what is your secret mystique?

Have your advanced technologists a mystique? So far I have found no evidence of finding any such, but only a sense of fate. 'We must go on and on and on.' Why? Curiosity drives us. Outwardly you conform to custom like solid, ethical citizens, as though unaware that the world now stands in far greater awe of you than of all living presidents, crowned heads, tycoons, scholars, and ecclesiasts. The world knows that you hold all lives in your hands; yet you insist on taking a purely objective view of the world's affairs. Moreover, you restrict your scientific ethics to the narrowest definition, that of factual accuracy in conducting and summarizing research. (The ethical rules used also, once, to stipulate the publication and exchange of all findings; but they have now been subordinated to so-called national interests.)

Your very modesty absolves you of reproach; you do not claim to be statesmen, executives, or spiritual advisers. And you exclude from your research all functions of the mind that may be directed towards its development not as a thinking machine—and here you have been taught its limits by computers of your own contrivance—but as a creative force capable of miraculous interventions in history.

I am grateful for your patient dedication, as Fate's agents, to the task of a *reductio ad absurdum*: the task of proving that intellect, when it tries to solve universal problems, can get only intellectual answers: to the effect that all hypotheses are of equal validity in this most anarchic of all possible universes. Never any answer commending itself to that other part of man's mind where is seated the emotional centre which (by some obscure exchange of vibrations with responsive emotional centres) generates an element popularly called Love; which, in turn (by some obscure biological chemistry), stimulates the creative faculties, rejuvenates the entire organism, and sympathetically affects a number of similar organisms attuned to it.

As the midwife told a young wife who complained of morning sickness: 'It will be worse before it's better, my duck, and then you'll have a lot of work on your hands.' But I am not a pessimist, and will now explain why: quoting, by your permission, from the now discredited Judaeo-Christian Bible.

The Bible was edited, during or shortly after the Exile, by a monotheistic and misogynous Guild of Prophets; they set themselves to delete all favourable reference to women who controlled men by their intuitive wisdom. Only one such case somehow escaped the censors: that of Deborah. She judged the Israelites when they were tributary to Jabin, King of Hazor, and issued oracles under a palm-tree (sacred to the Goddess Anatha) rather than under Jehovah's holy terebinth. *Deborah* means 'bee', and 'bee' was the honorary title of all oracular priestesses in Greater Greece and Syria.

The name of Deborah's husband is mentioned; but he was a cypher. She summoned an Ephraimite named Barak, and gave him instructions for leading a revolt of Zebulon, Issachar and Naphtali—although Israel had long been totally disarmed by Sisera, Jabin's commander-in-chief, who could bring 900 iron chariots into the field. Barak replied: 'If you join us on Mount Tabor, I will obey.' She told him: 'If you need my presence there, I will come; but by bargaining, you have forfeited the glory of killing Sisera with your own hand. A woman shall now win it.' So the battle was won; and Jael, in defiance of her husband Heber, Jabin's ally, took a typical woman's revenge on Sisera, for which she was subsequently praised by Deborah. As for the 900 iron chariots—Deborah and Barak afterwards sang together in triumph: 'The River Kishon swept them away; that ancient river, the River Kishon!'

No release from the present impasse can come, in my view, except from a Barak who has put himself under Deborah's orders. *Barak* means 'lightning', but is associated with *báraka*, or 'blessedness' that comes from divine Wisdom. Potential Deborahs are not uncommon even today, but the Jabins and Siseras make every effort to limit their activities and sap their self-reliance. The Deborahs either resign themselves to marriage, or commit some spectacular form of suicide, or are confined to the psychotic wards of mental hospitals. It is the Baraks who are missing from the scene, or who fail to answer their summons.

Goethe prophesied the eventual rejuvenation of our world by a going-back to Nature. If, however, he was right, 'Nature' must be interpreted not as *natura naturata*, 'Nature as scientifically observed', but as *natura naturans*, 'creative Nature', which implies the power of love. Nor must love be read as grand-scale international philanthropy; but as a personal understanding between Barak, the male mind, and Deborah, the female mind. This alone can lift humanity out of the morass where intellectual arrogance has sunk it and develop the so-called supernatural powers of which both sexes are capable.

Now, the Irish Muse-goddess Brigid was threefold. She watched not only over poets—a term that included musicians, historians, story-tellers and astronomers—but over every kind of craftsman: from the illuminator to the architect; and over all physicians. Such natural sciences as astronomy, chemistry and navigation also came under her loving care, and were shared among her devotees. Their original discoveries—those inspired leaps in the dark—

became craft mysteries. In ancient Greece, the Goddess Athene ruled every art and natural science, until ousted by the upstart God Apollo. Apollo was the first to patronize unnatural science—science as an intellectual perversion, science for the sake of science.

If Goethe's prophecy of the world's rejuvenation is to be fulfilled, and if my Deborah-Barak analogy holds, then the Barak chosen to deliver Israel from Sisera's 900 iron chariots must necessarily be an original scientist who, meditating among the woods of Mount Ephraim, has suddenly been inspired by the Goddess's flash of lightning. He will see that the future of thought does not lie in the cosmical nonsense-region of electronic computers, but in the Paradisal region of what he will not be ashamed to call 'magic'. He must obey Deborah's summons to the palm-tree, follow her irrational instructions, trust her implicitly, and allow full weight to the scientifically imponderable. And the River Kishon will sweep away Sisera's 900 iron chariots. The more prodigally numerous those iron chariots, and the more select the tribesmen commanded by Barak—observe that Deborah records 'out of Zebulon came they that handle the pen of a writer'—then the more certain his victory. That sudden destructive flood of the Kishon's very small stream, a cosmic coincidence that upset the logistics of Sisera's Pentagon, was naturally ordained by the poetic bond between Deborah and Barak. 'And the land had rest for forty years. . . .'

Forgive me!

Three Oxford Lectures on Poetry

Michaelmas Term, 1962

Some Instances of Poetic Vulgarity

A French editor invited me the other day to join a symposium in praise of Robert Browning. At the risk of seeming a snob, I excused myself on the ground of his vulgarity, adding: 'This does not mean that Browning wrote in a non-academic style for the larger public, as one might call Victor Hugo vulgar, but that he was clearly no gentleman. The Muse has, of course, shown equal favour to poets of every rank and condition: to King Henry VIII; to the Earl of Surrey; to Sir Walter Raleigh; to John Clare, the Northamptonshire peasant; to William Davies, the South Welsh tramp; to John Keats, whose father was a groom; and to William Shakespeare, whose father was a wholesale provision dealer. Therefore to call Browning clearly no gentleman, and seemingly introduce class-barriers into a classless society, implies that he was clearly no poet either.'

What *is* vulgarity? Ruskin defined it as a 'deadness of heart and body resulting from prolonged and especially from inherited, conditions of degeneracy'. What he calls 'vulgar' I should call 'banal'. There is a livelier, likeable sort of vulgarity: the strident, active, healthy, uninhibited, generous vulgarity of the Edwardian music-hall, or of New York vaudeville when Teddy Roosevelt was President. But vulgarity as a critical term means, as a rule, someone's swaggering attempt to be at ease in a class or group with different customs and taboos from his own.

Vulgaritas carried no social stigma in ancient Rome, once the power of the aristocratic families had been broken. Gaius Petronius's Trimalchio was rich, insensitive and uneducated; but as a priest of Augustus, he felt thoroughly at ease in bullying and looking down on his better bred and less successful fellow-townsmen. Indeed, I read him as Petronius's satire on the Emperor Nero who, though brought up anyhow under the care of a barber and a Circus dancer, stood high above all social criticism. 'Vulgarity', however, in English usage, is historically associated with *vulgus mobile*, 'the easily-moved crowd', from which comes the word *mob*. The mob, or 'mobility', were, for the three established 'Estates', rabble without patrons or clients, without representation, responsibility, or convictions: the objects of either scorn or pity.

Adult suffrage, two world wars, Labour Governments, compulsory education and crippling death-duties have gradually blurred social distinctions in Britain. Sportsmanship is now the one universally recognized moral virtue; all sportsmen rank as gentlemen. The servant class has disappeared; a skilled manual worker often earns more than a university graduate; and the diminished importance given to all but technical accomplishments in education encourages the spread of what used to be called 'mob-taste' even among persons of royal blood. The *Daily Sketch* and *Daily Mirror* hail it as 'the popular touch'.

School anthologies harbour countless examples of vulgar verse, still fed to children as worthy of admiration. Take Browning's *Marching Along*, his ballad of 'Kentish Sir Byng', a Cavalier who fought in the Civil War. Browning, the son of a Bank of England clerk, was by birth and environment an enthusiastic crop-headed Ironside. Yet here he casts himself for the part of a great-hearted, long-tressed Cavalier:

> Kentish Sir Byng stood for his King,
> Bidding the crop-headed Parliament swing:
> And, pressing a troop unable to stoop
> And see the rogues flourish and honest folk droop,

Marched them along, fifty-score strong,
Great-hearted gentlemen, singing this song.

God for King Charles! Pym and such carles
To the Devil that prompts 'em their treasonable parles!
Cavaliers up! Lips from the cup,
Hands from the pasty, nor bite take nor sup
Till you're—

> CHORUS: Marching along, fifty-score strong,
> Great-hearted gentlemen, singing this song.

We read that Sir Byng pressed 'great-hearted gentle-men' for the King's service. Browning used *pressed* because it had a more urgent sound than 'raised', yet 'pressing' implies forcibly overcoming their reluctance to serve the King—a trait, however, of which he reports them incapable. *Troop*, *stoop* and *droop* all seem chosen to rhyme with each other, though *troop* probably occurred to Browning first. Being neither a soldier nor a historian, he did not know what strength a 'troop' would have had in King Charles's day; but to glorify Sir Byng (a fictitious character, perhaps short for 'Browning', and rhymed with *King*) he put it at 1,000 Cavaliers, or two cavalry regiments. Sir Byng finds them all together by some happy accident, armed and accoutred, at a gigantic wine-and-pasty picnic. Before grace can be said, Sir Byng's apt rhyme about King Charles, Pym's carles, and their treasonable parles, provokes them to rise up, still hungry and thirsty, and march off to battle with no better preparation than a song. Talk of the Pied Piper of Hamelin! As the *Dictionary of National Biography* notes: 'Browning's poems everywhere attested unflinching optimism.' *Marching Along* is a day-dream of glory, doubtless provoked (like the no less unhistorical *How They Brought the Good News from Aix to Ghent*) by the sensuous rhythm of Browning's early-morning horseback constitutional in the Park; and undeniably vulgar.

Here is Browning at sea: a poem worked up from stray diary jottings:

HOME-THOUGHTS, FROM THE SEA

Nobly, nobly Cape Saint Vincent to the North-west died away;
Sunset ran, one glorious blood-red, reeking into Cadiz Bay;
Bluish 'mid the burning water, full in face Trafalgar lay;
In the dimmest North-east distance dawned Gibraltar grand and gray;
'Here and here did England help me: how can I help England?'
    —say,
Whoso turns as I, this evening, turn to God to praise and pray,
While Jove's planet rises yonder, silent over Africa.

Nine readers out of ten will identify 'this evening' and 'the burning water' with the sunset at Cadiz; supposing that Trafalgar lay on the Spanish coast opposite Cadiz Bay, Gibraltar to the North-east where the dawn would presently break, and Cape St Vincent some miles to the North-west. . . . A glance at the map will surprise them. Cape St Vincent lies 120 miles almost due west from Cadiz; Trafalgar thirty miles south of Cadiz; and Gibraltar round the corner in the Mediterranean. Sentimental allusions to Nelson's victories at St Vincent and Trafalgar, and to Lord Heathfield's earlier defence of Gibraltar would, Browning reckoned, make patriotic schoolboys ambitious of joining the Senior Service. The glorious blood-red sunset that reeked into Cadiz Bay is a daringly phrased reminder of Drake's surprise attack— against Royal orders—on the Spanish fleet in 1587. Needing a purple last line, Browning solemnly records that Jove's planet rose silent over Africay—to rhyme with *pray*. Did he expect it to sing *Rule, Britannia*?

Browning's vulgarity is a link between Thomas Campbell's and Rudyard Kipling's. Campbell, the youngest of an impoverished Scottish merchant's eleven children, won verse-prizes at Glasgow University, and was 'discovered' by the same Henry Mackenzie who had discovered Burns. *The Battle of Copenhagen*, *Ye Mariners of England* (not *Scotland*), and other patriotic songs, earned him a Government pension. Though his hope of political advancement was frustrated by the death of his patron Fox, he lived comfortably from his patriotic verse throughout the Napoleonic Wars; and found it hard to make ends meet only during the long period of peace that followed Waterloo. Then he addressed his trumpet-calls to other nations.

To the Greeks (1822):

> Again to the battle, Achaians,
> Our hearts bid the tyrants' defiance. . . . [*sic*]

To the Spaniards (1823):

> How rings each sparkling Spanish brand!
>   There's music in its rattle,
> And gay, as for a saraband
>   We gird us for the battle,
>   Follow, follow,
> To the glorious revelry
>   When the sabres bristle
>   And the death shots whistle.

While encouraging these Spaniards, was Campbell aware that the saraband is a slow, melancholy dance, most unsuitable for the gorgeous revelry of battle—its steps being two forward and three back? Did he even care?

To the Poles (1831):

> And have I lived to see thee, sword in hand
> Uprise again, immortal Polish land?

To the Germans (1832):

> The spirit of Britannia
>   Invokes, across the main,
> Her sister Alemannia
>   To burst the tyrant's chain.

Campbell had served briefly as a volunteer when England's shores were threatened by Bonaparte; 'but oh! what fagging work this volunteering is!' he wrote; and having had a grandstand view of real war at Ratisbon— from a monastery garden near the battlefield—felt no inclination to go overseas. He confided to a friend: 'I stood with the good monks of St James to overlook a charge of Kleinau's cavalry upon the French. This proved the most important epoch of my life in point of impressions, but they are so horrible to my memory that I study to banish them.' Safe back in London, however, he could write:

> The combat deepens. On, ye brave
> Who rush to glory or the grave!
> Wave, Munich, all thy banners wave
> And charge with all thy chivalry!

Which reminds me of a vulgar old song:

> When the bugle calls we shall march to war
> As we did in days gone by.
> When the bugle calls, we shall march, march, march,
> April, May, June and July.
> When the bugle calls we shall march to war
> And not a man will fear it—
> And I don't care how soon the bloody bugle calls,
> So long as I don't hear it.

Campbell's *Wounded Hussar* had swept the country in 1797. A really successful patriotic poem should have a long, rolling metre, assisted by such feminine rhymes as *beaming, streaming; cherished, perished; story, glory;* and be utterly nonsensical in plot:

> Alone to the banks of the dark-rolling Danube
> Fair Adelaide hied when the battle was o'er:
> 'O, whither,' she cried, 'hast thou wandered, my lover?
> Or here dost thou welter and bleed on the shore?'

60

'What voice did I hear? 'twas my Henry that sighed!'
All mournful she hastened; nor wandered she far,
When, bleeding and low, on the heath she descried
By the light of the moon her poor wounded Hussar!

From his bosom that heaved the last torrent was streaming,
And pale was his visage, deep marked with a scar!
And dim was his eye, once expressively beaming,
That melted in love and that kindled in war!

For triumphs like this, Campbell was three times
elected Rector of Glasgow University; and buried, on
July 3, 1844, in Westminster Abbey, at the very centre of
Poets' Corner. Present were Lord Macaulay, Lockhart,
Brougham, Sir Robert Peel, the Duke of Argyle, and a
guard of grateful Polish nobles, one of whom sprinkled on
the coffin a handful of earth from the grave of the patriot
Kozciuzcko. . . .

Kipling's uncertainty is explained by his sense of not-
belonging—in an Anglo-Indian society where, as a
Bombay-born journalist without either a settled English
background or a university education, he ranked below
the youngest second-lieutenant in the tattiest battalion of
the Indian Army. Worse, he was a Methodist, not
Church of England. Yet Kipling had a quick journalistic
eye and ear. Soon he revenged himself by interpreting
British India to the stay-at-homes, with a good deal less
sympathy for *pukka sahibs* than for Privates Mulvaney,
Orth'ris and company, the regimental water-carrier
Gunga Din, and the otherwise under-privileged. At the
age of forty-one, he was awarded the Nobel Prize.
Kipling claimed to be a no-nonsense poet, a mouthpiece
of the common people, who swept away academic hum-
bug. His *Boots, boots, boots, boots!* is now the best-known
English poem in the Soviet Union. But when the Establishment beckoned, he followed: at last squarely identify-

ing himself with the Lords and Masters, rather than the 'lesser breeds within the Law', and bravely shouldering the White Man's Burden.

Kipling became the unofficial poet laureate of the British Empire just before its liquidation. He missed the official appointment only because he had earned Queen Victoria's displeasure by alluding to her as 'the Widow of Windsor'. Like Browning and Campbell, he weltered vicariously in gore, as in the climax to his fictional *Ballad of the Clampherdown*:

> . . . . It was our war-ship *Clampherdown*,
>   Swung round upon the tide,
> Her two dumb guns glared south and north,
> And the blood and the bubbling steam ran forth,
>   And she ground the cruiser's side.
>
> 'Captain,' they cry, 'the fight is done,
>   They bid you send your sword.'
> And he answered: 'Grapple her, stern and bow.
> They have asked for the steel. They shall have it now;
>   Out cutlasses and board!'
>
> It was our war-ship *Clampherdown*
>   Spewed up four hundred men;
> And the scalded stokers yelped delight
> As they rolled in the waist and heard the fight
>   Stamp o'er their steel-walled pen.
>
> They cleared the cruiser end to end,
>   From conning-tower to hold.
> They fought as they fought in Nelson's fleet;
> They were stripped to the waist, they were bare to the feet,
>   As it was in the days of old.

I could quote nothing from all English literature that transcended in vulgar bloody-mindedness the third of these stanzas. The stokers, no doubt ignoble Lascars, unfit to wield a white man's cutlass, are left below decks; and their screams of pain as salt water reaches the boilers and steam scalds them, are jovially interpreted as yelps of delight! 'Bubbling', by the way, has been transferred for the sake of euphony from 'blood' to 'steam'.

A frequent sign of poetic vulgarity is the use of Biblical language to heighten trivial passages. Kipling specialized not only in grandiose addresses to the Lord God of Hosts, but also in dewy-eyed quotation from the New Testament. The affected simplicity of *Gethsemane* shows him at his lowest:

> The Garden called Gethsemane
>   In Picardy it was,
> And there the people came to see
>   The English soldiers pass.

> We used to pass—we used to pass
>   Or halt, as it might be,
> And ship our masks in case of gas
>   Beyond Gethsemane.

> The Garden called Gethsemane,
>   It held a pretty lass,
> But all the time she talked to me
>   I prayed my cup might pass.

> The officer sat on the chair,
>   The men lay on the grass,
> And all the time we halted there
>   I prayed my cup might pass.

> It didn't pass—it didn't pass—
>   It didn't pass from me.
> I drank it when we met the gas
>   Beyond Gethsemane.

Why, at a period in the First World War subsequent to the issue of gas-masks, as opposed to 'respirators' (probably the early summer of 1916), Picardy peasants were still interested in watching the British soldiers pass—'or halt, as it might be'; and why they continued to occupy an area so close to the German lines that gas-masks were habitually shipped there; and why the pretty lass singled out this Christ-like private soldier for her French monologue, when all he could do was lie on the grass in an agony, shut his eyes and pray against gas; and why, for that matter, he *did* get gassed in the end—must remain mysteries. Perhaps the practical Picardaise wanted him to stop praying *un petit moment*, and make sure that his mask had its eye-pieces properly secured. . . .

Non-scholarly pretence at scholarship is another form of poetic vulgarity, used throughout Browning's *Sordello*, though he quotes only the Classics and a little Italian—not Chinese, Sanskrit or Provençal, like his modernist successors.

It is natural for young people to gather in a crowd, play the same games, use the same jargon; and if some physical misfortune or social disadvantage (rather than a rare extra gift of the spirit) differentiates one of them from his fellows, this often tempts him to some sort of megalomaniac over-compensation. Byron knew and regretted the colossal vulgarity which he shrouded by a cloak of aloof grandeur. It was a studious vulgarity: cosmetics and curl-papers tended his elegant beauty; an ingenious, though synthetic, verse technique smoothed his cynical Spenserian stanzas. But he had unexpectedly come into a peerage and an estate while still 'wee Georgie Gordon with the feetsies'—whom his hysterical and unladylike mother used to send limping round the corner from her cheap Aberdeen lodgings to buy two-penny-worth of 'blue ruin'; and whom, at the age of nine, a nymphomaniac Calvinist housemaid had violently debauched.

SOME INSTANCES OF POETIC VULGARITY

His unease was prodigious. As he himself confesses in
Childe Harold:

> His cup was quaff'd too quickly, and he found
> The dregs were wormwood; but he fill'd again,
> And from a purer fount, on holier ground,
> And deem'd its spring perpetual; but in vain!
> Still round him clung invisibly a chain
> Which gall'd for ever, fettering though unseen,
> And heavy though it clank'd not; worn with pain,
> Which pined although it spoke not, and grew keen,
> Entering with every step to look through many a scene.

Shelley noted in a letter to Peacock:

> Lord Byron is an exceedingly interesting person and, as such,
> is it not to be regretted that he is a slave to the vilest and most
> vulgar prejudices, and as mad as a hatter?

Byron adored no Muse, but acted as male Muse to
scores of infatuated women who, like Lady Caroline
Lamb, knew that he was 'mad, bad, dangerous to know',
adding: 'His beautiful face is my fate.' I pair Byron and
Nero as the two most dangerously talented bounders of all
time.

Swinburne's was an inverted vulgarity. One of his
grandfathers had been an admiral; the other an earl.
After a healthy North Country childhood, he went on to
Eton and Oxford. Later, he tried to edge, not into high
society, but into the 'fleshy' Bohemian set of pre-
Raphaelite poets and painters. For them he celebrated the
roses and raptures of vice; though, whereas Byron could
wearily boast of having enjoyed over two hundred
mistresses and scores of catamites, the impotent eroticism
of Swinburne's verse, even when it celebrated merely
vegetable Nature, leaves a worse taste in the mouth than
Childe Harold:

BY THE NORTH SEA

A land that is lonelier than ruin;
   A sea that is stranger than death;
Far fields that a rose never blew in,
   Wan waste where the winds lack breath;
Waste endless and boundless and flowerless
   But of marsh-blossoms fruitless as free;
Where earth lies exhausted, as powerless
   To strive with the sea.

Far flickers the flight of the swallows,
   Far flutters the weft of the grass
Spun dense over desolate hollows
   More pale than the clouds as they pass;
Thick woven as the weft of a witch is
   Round the heart of a thrall that hath sinned
Whose youth and the wrecks of its riches
   Are waifs on the wind.

Nineteenth-century poetic vulgarity is characterized by over-alliteration, ingenious rhymes—such as *blew in* and *ruin*; *riches, which is*—and a reckless disregard of prose sense. In Swinburne's windless, endless, boundless waste, the weft of grass, he says, fluttered far—spun dense over desolate hollows that were paler than the passing clouds, and thick woven as the weft of a witch around the heart of a sinner whose youthful charms had become like waifs in the wind. . . . But did a wind flutter the grass and drive the clouds, or did it not? And how can a waste region of England adjacent to the North Sea be endless and boundless? And how can a weft be *spun?* And if the grass had been spun densely over the desolate hollows, who could tell whether they were as pale as the clouds that passed? And how pale were the clouds anyhow? And how thick a weft does a witch weave around the sinner's heart? And how do fruitless marsh-flowers spread themselves freely across the exhausted earth?

SOME INSTANCES OF POETIC VULGARITY

Keats, though no gentleman either by birth or education, had a genuine instinct for poetry and poetic principle; and the close attention he paid to craftsmanship made him recognize vulgarity in others and, as a rule, avoid it himself. He particularly lamented the fate of Burns:

Poor unfortunate fellow—how sad it is when a luxurious imagination is obliged in self-defence to deaden its delicacy in vulgarity, and in things attainable—that it may not have leisure to go mad after things which are not attainable.

Vulgarity in religious dress is insidious; and Keats, who in this letter has been denouncing the hypocritical Kirk, was evidently referring to Burn's *Cottar's Saturday Night,* an 'unco-guid' set-piece that contradicted his natural randiness and imitated Robert Fergusson's more authentic *The Farmer's Wife.*

Almost every poet starts to write before finding his own voice, and puffs out his borrowed feathers. Every theatrical impersonation, every political, theological, or philosophical hand-out passed off as his own, is a vulgarity. The writing of true poems happens so unpredictably that the poet is beset by the temptation to write when not in the mood. He may think that this can be induced by withdrawing to a glade or quiet, book-filled study, or by violent adventure among corsairs, alguazils, barmecides, and their modern equivalents. It cannot be.

No poet has yet solved the main problem: how to maintain the gift of certitude. Always to be in love: that is one recommendation. To treat money and fame with equal nonchalance, is another. To remain independent, is a third. To prize personal honour, is a fourth. To make the English language one's constant study, is a fifth. . . . Yet lightning strikes where and when it wills. No one ever knows. It is easy to take up a pen at random and plead:

'I'm just keeping my hand in.' But nine-tenths of what passes as English poetry is the product of either careerism, or keeping one's hand in: a choice between vulgarity and banality.

Technique in Poetry

God, according to a Hebrew myth, promised our father Adam the helpmate he needed, and invited him to watch while the divine fingers built up a woman's anatomy from primeval sludge. They extemporized bones, tissues, muscles, blood, teeth, brains and glandular secretions, wove them neatly together, co-ordinated their functions, covered the whole ingenious apparatus with the smoothest of cuticles, and embellished it with tufts of hair in selected places. This technical demonstration caused Adam such disgust that, when the First Eve stood up in all her beauty and smiled at him, he turned his back on her. God therefore removed the First Eve and behaved with greater circumspection: He formed the Second Eve from Adam's rib while he slept, then ordered the Archangel Michael to plait her hair and adorn her in bridal array. Adam woke and was enchanted.

I inherit Adam's mistrust of creative technique. It is grammarians, not poets, who lay down the rules of prosody, name metres, list different varieties of poetic licence—deducing them from Greek, Latin, Italian or French practice—as of universal application. English criticism began in Tudor times with the grammarians; and though some, such as George Puttenham, realized that English poetry had its own wayward genius, different from that of the Romance languages, they nevertheless agreed that it must be intellectually disciplined and dedicated to certain social uses. Among these, Puttenham instances the Reporting of the Famous Lives of Princes, the Reproval of Vice, the Treatment of Honest and Profitable Sciences; Solemn Rejoicings at Marriages;

Memorials to the Dead. Puttenham links poetic art so securely with the art of rhetoric that, when he has discussed the mathematical rules of metre and proportion, which ensure sweet and tuneful sounds, he next turns to the problem of poetic ornament:

And as we see in these great Mesdames of honour, who be they never so comely and beautiful, yet if they want their courtly habilements, or at least such other apparel as custom and civility have ordained to cover their naked bodies, would be half-ashamed or greatly out of countenance to be seen in that sort, and perchance do then think themselves more amiable in every man's eye when they be in their richest attire—suppose of silks or tissues and costly embroideries—than when they go in cloth or in any plain and simple apparel. Even so cannot our Poesie show itself either gallant or gorgeous if any limb be left naked and bare and not clad in his kindly clothes and colours, such as may convey them somewhat out of sight from the common course of ordinary speech and capacity of the vulgar judgement, and yet, being artificially handled, must needs yield it much more beauty and commendation. This Ornament we speak of is given to it by figures and figurative speeches, which be the flowers, as it were, and colours that a Poet setteth upon his language of art, as the embroiderer doth his stones and pearls and passments of gold upon the stuff of a princely garment. . . .

Ornament, as such, should not concern poets, although completely naked poems spring only from extreme passion in love or war. It is true that beautiful women, because of 'custom or civility'—not to mention variations of climate—wear clothes as a rule: yet, if truly beautiful and not mere lumps of handsome flesh, they dress for their own pleasure, rather than let fashion-designers (even the Archangel Michael himself) bedizen them for Adam's gratification. And any jewel a woman wears is not mere ornament but a chosen extension of her inner loveliness.

Grammarians insist that a simple idea may be so ornamented by artifice as to become poetic, and that the reader must applaud the ingenuity of its transformation. Poetical artifice entered our Universities from Rome by way of France; Ovid and Virgil were the masters on whom all students must model themselves. Ovid wrote in the *Fasti*:

> Tres ubi luciferos veniens praemiserit Eos
> Tempora nocturnis aequa diurna feres.
> Inde quater pastor saturos ubi clauserit hoedos
> Canuerint herbae rore recente quater,
> Janus adorandus, cumque hoc Concordia mitis. . . .

When the breaking dawn shall have sent before her three light-bearing days, thou wilt have the hours of day equal to those of night; and when from this the shepherd shall four times have penned his well-fed kids, four times the grass become white with fresh-fallen dew, then Janus and with him Mild Concord will demand adoration. . . .

In simple English: 'Three days later comes the vernal equinox; after four more, the feasts of Janus and Concord will be celebrated.' Note the superfluousness of the adjectives—*breaking* dawn, *well-fed* kids, *fresh-fallen* dew, *mild* Concord. Every dawn *breaks*: and even if all the shepherd's kids were not *well fed*, their hungry bleatings would not affect the Calendar; dew is always *fresh-fallen*, and Concord always *mild*. In any case, Ovid was writing not for shepherds, but for Augustus's City courtiers—few of whom can ever have seen the inside of a goat pen.

Sir Philip Sidney, in his *Apology for Poetry*, accepts this whole cosmetic parlour of Classical verse-technique as necessary for the production of rich conceits that guide man's soul to moral virtue, courage and erudition; adding, however:

Certainly I must confess my own barbarousness. I never heard the old song of Percy and Douglas [*Chevy Chase*] that I found not my heart moved more than by a trumpet; and yet is it sung but by some blind crowder with no rougher voice than rude; which, being so evil apparelled in the dust and cobwebs of that uncivil age, what would it work if trimmed with the gorgeous eloquence of Pindar?

Now, Pindar could never have begun a poem with:

> The stout Earl of Northumberland
> A vow to God did make. . . .

but would have written:

O Queenly Muse, our Mother, come, I beseech thee, on the festal day of the Omnipotent Christchild who bountifully redeemed us from sin: come visiting the spacious halls of our impregnable New Castle that beetles in majesty above the goodly Tynian water. For lo, youthful craftsmen of honey-sweet triumphal songs, skilled also in laments, there attend in long desire for thy voice. Various deeds thirst for various rewards, yet the hunting of high-stepping, lotus-cropping deer that rove the rugged Cheviotian hills, calleth beyond all things for the meed of song, especially when mighty champions contend together in honour, each assuring for himself the certain glory of carrying home in well-wrought horse-drawn wains tasty haunches of unnumbered antlered ones.

It would have taken Pindar a whole page to trim with gorgeous eloquence such stanzas as these:

> It began upon a Monynday
>   Ere daylight did appear
> The drivers through the woodës went
>   To raise the fallow deer.
>
> The bowmen cleft them to the hearts,
>   As down the brae they came,
> And greyhounds through the greves did run—
>   To them it was good game.

Two centuries later, Dr Johnson wrote about *Chevy Chase*:

Addison descended now and then to lower disquisitions than his praise of Milton. By a serious display of the beauties of *Chevy Chase* he exposed himself to the ridicule of Wagstaff and to the contempt of Dennis who, considering the fundamental position that *Chevy Chase* pleases, and ought to please, because it is natural, observes: 'There is a way of deviating from nature by bombast or tumour, which soars above nature and enlarges images beyond their real bulk; by affectation which forsakes nature in quest of something unsuitable; and by imbecility, which degrades nature by faintliness and diminution, by obscuring its appearances and weakening its effects. In *Chevy Chase* there is not much of either bombast or affectation, but there is a chill, lifeless imbecility. The story cannot possibly be told in a manner that shall make less impression in the mind.'

The Classicists thus ask us to choose between the 'chill and lifeless imbecility' of *Chevy Chase* and such 'supreme excellence' as Addison's *Letter from Italy* which, Dr Johnson says, has 'always been praised but never beyond its merit, being more correct, with less appearance of labour and more elegant with less ambition of ornament, than any of his other poems'.

A LETTER FROM ITALY
(To the Right Hon. Charles Lord Halifax, 1701)

While you, my lord, the rural shades admire,
And from Britannia's public posts retire,
Nor longer, her ungrateful sons to please,
For their advantage sacrifice your ease;
Me into foreign realms my fate conveys
Through nations fruitful of immortal lays,
Where the soft season and inviting clime
Conspire to trouble your repose with rhyme. . . . etc.

*

I have elsewhere explained the difference between Apollonian poetry and Muse poetry. That Pindar and Addison claim to have the Muse in their pockets, complicates the situation. Yet the truth is that *Chevy Chase* moved Sir Philip Sidney's heart more than a trumpet because the unknown rude crowder who composed it was himself so moved; and that the Apollonians decry all emotional impulses which have not been modified and ennobled, after a grounding in the humanities, by the acquisition of Classical technique. Technique should not be equated with craftsmanship. Technique is psychological know-how. The technician assumes that poems can be constructed like explosive missiles and aimed at a given target; he despises mere craftsmen for their intellectual sloth. Eliot, Pound, and the later Yeats (still praised by English and American literary journals as the 'real masters') have technique; Hardy and Frost had only craftsmanship.

Technique ignores the factor of magic; craftsmanship presupposes it. A journeyman, after seven years as apprentice, will get the feel of his materials and learn what quiet miracles can be done with them. A small part of this knowledge is verbally communicable; the rest is incommunicable—except to fellow-craftsmen who already possess it. The technician's disregard of this inexplicable element, magic, in painting, sculpture, medicine, music and poetry—on the ground that it cannot be demonstrated under laboratory conditions—accounts for the present dismal decline in all arts. A true poem is best regarded as already existing before it has been composed: with composition as the act of deducing its entirety from a single key phrase that swims into the poet's mind.

*

Here are two well-known pieces of Tennyson's, *The Eagle* and *Move Eastward, Happy Earth*, printed on the same page in his *Collected Poems* and forced on me, when

I was seven or eight years old, as works of genius. *The Eagle* is subtitled 'A Fragment', suggesting that a longer poem went wrong and that he destroyed all but six sound lines. Whenever this happens to a poet, he should justify by careful craftsmanship the publication of what is salved. But has Tennyson done so?

> He clasps the crag with crooked hands;
> Close to the sun in lonely lands,
> Ring'd with the azure world, he stands.
>
> The wrinkled sea beneath him crawls;
> He watches from his mountain walls,
> And like a thunderbolt he falls.

My minimum requirement of a poem is that it should make prose sense as well as poetic sense; one main difference between prose and poetry being that prose engages only a small part of the reader's attention. Ideally, a poem should induce in him the same trance of heightened sensibility under which the poet wrote, and make him aware of all the multiple meanings that stretch out in vistas from it. Here, Tennyson's technique has been deliberately impressionistic—he has, in fact, taken no pains to say what he means—and, although his resonant voice with the slight Norfolk burr might have persuaded his hearers that these two stanzas make prose sense (the ear being easily deceived), the reading eye rejects them.

Persistent alliteration pleases children, who enjoy 'One old ox opening oysters', and 'Two toads terribly tired, trying to trot to Tilbury'. And it pleased simple Anglo-Saxons:

> With Vandals I was and with Vaerns and Vikings;
> With Saxons I was and with Syegs and Swordsmen;
> With Franks I was, with Frisians and Frumtings. . . .

But when, in a Victorian three-line rhyming stanza, four c's appear in a row—*clasp, crag, crooked* and *close*—fol-

lowed by the two l's of *lonely lands*, we expect the last line
to yield an important and equally alliterative statement:

> He clasps the crag with crooked hands
> Close to the sun in lonely lands. . . .

Yet,

> Ring'd with the azure world he stands . . .

disappoints expectation, and adds nothing to the picture.
Since the eagle perches on his crag close to the sun, a background of blue sky has already been presumed. Besides, it is
not the *world* which is blue, but only the sky. And why 'he
clasps the crag with crooked *hands*'? Though few men are
born with prehensile feet, 'hands' might still have passed
muster in a portrait of this humanized eagle, had Tennyson not followed it with 'he stands'. If the eagle stands on
his hands, then his wings must necessarily be feet. . . .

Once one thinks along these lines, the poem collapses.
Crooked is unnecessary: eagles' claws are always crooked.
Lands is seen to be a rhyme chosen to go with *hands* and
stands; for the eagle can stand only in one land, not
several. To present him as 'close to the sun' is hardly fair
—what are a few hundred feet, compared with 92,000,000
miles! Nor is he even flying high above the mountain;
but grounded on a crag. . . .

Azure is a purely heraldic term for 'blue', and if
Tennyson thought of the eagle as a heraldic charge—
*Azure: below a sun in its splendour or, an eagle of the
same, ungled and langed argent*—he should have made
this clear. *Ringed with azure* is not the language of
heraldry.

> The wrinkled sea beneath him crawls;
> He watches from his mountain walls,
> And like a thunderbolt he falls. . . .

Why is the bird's attention concentrated on the sea? Is he
perhaps a sea-eagle, watching for fish? *Crawls* may mean

76

that from a great height waves appear to move slowly; but since *wrinkles* are by definition static, *crawls* must have been put there for the rhyme. And unless we are told exactly what the eagle is watching, his fall could have been as accidental as was, say, Eutychus's when Paul's sermon sent him to sleep and he crashed on to the street from an upper window. . . . Tennyson has a vague sense, perhaps, of the eagle as a royal bird mythologically entitled—like Solar Jove, his master—to a blue nimbus and a thunderbolt. . . . If so, he does not make the point. He would have done better with:

JOVE'S EAGLE

Charged on an azure field, with claws
Grasping a crag, he overawes
(Like Jove himself) the doves and daws.

Silently watches from his walls
What swims the sea, what flies, what crawls—
Ere like a thunderbolt he falls.

This is still not a poem. I have indulged Tennyson by granting him his Victorian *daws* and his *Ere*; nor do I much like the similarity of these two sets of rhymes; but at least the verses now make immediate prose sense and would serve well enough as an anthology piece.

*

Now for its companion verse:

Move eastward, happy earth, and leave
Yon orange sunset waning slow:
From fringes of the faded eve,
O, happy planet, eastward go;
Till over thy dark shoulder glow
Thy silver sister-world, and rise
To glass herself in dewy eyes
That watch me from the glen below.

> Ah, bear me with thee, smoothly borne,
> Dip forward under starry light,
> And move me to my marriage-morn,
> And round again to happy night.

The gist is: 'I shall be so happy when the sunset has ended; when tonight's moon has come and gone, and morning is here, and I am married to Maud, and—oh, tomorrow night!'

Nobody can put this poem right. It would have to be re-written as a popular song:

> O tomorrow night,
> O tomorrow night,
> I'll be so happy when today is done,
> And I've said goodbye to the dear old sun. . . .

That an eager lover should apostrophize the weather to be fine on his wedding day, and the birds to wake him early, and the countryside to rejoice, is understandable. Lovers always take the weather personally. But when Earth is begged to dip forward and carry the poet along with smooth and careful portage for another twenty-four hours or so . . . !

> Move eastward, happy earth. . . .

and

> O, happy planet, eastward go!

though parallel orders, are far from explicit. 'Eastward of what must I dip, Mr Tennyson?' Mother Earth has a right to ask.

> . . . Till over thy dark shoulder glow
> Thy silver sister-world, and rise
> To glass herself in dewy eyes
> That watch me from the glen below.

78

> Ah, bear me with thee, smoothly borne,
>   Dip forward under starry light,
> And move me to my marriage-morn,
>   And round again to happy night.

'Thy sister-world' refers to the moon; but just whose dewy eyes are watching Tennyson from the glen below is a puzzle. Perhaps a couple of small lakes? If so, why dewy? Glens may be dewy, but not lakes. And why are they watching? Are they perhaps Maud's eyes? If so, what is she doing down there in the damp glen at this late hour?

*

Shelley is another culprit:

TO A SKYLARK

> Hail to thee, blithe Spirit!
>   Bird thou never wert,
> That from Heaven, or near it,
>   Pourest thy full heart
> In profuse strains of unpremeditated art.

> Higher still and higher
>   From the earth thou springest
> Like a cloud of fire;
>   The deep blue thou wingest,
> And singing still dost soar, and soaring ever singest.

> In the golden lightning
>   Of the sunken sun,
> O'er which clouds are bright'ning,
>   Thou dost float and run;
> Like an unbodied joy whose race is just begun.

> The pale purple even
>   Melts around thy flight;
> Like a star of Heaven,
>   In the broad daylight
> Thou art unseen, but yet I hear thy shrill delight,

79

Like a poet hidden
   In the light of thought,
Singing hymns unbidden,
   Till the world is wrought
To sympathy with hopes and fears it heeded not:

Chorus Hymeneal,
   Or triumphal chant,
Matched with thine would be all
   But an empty vaunt,
A thing wherein we feel there is a hidden want.

What objects are the fountains
   Of thy happy strain?
What fields of waves, or mountains?
   What shapes of sky or plain?
What love of thine own kind? what ignorance of pain?

It is a temptation to let Shelley off; but *To A Skylark*
ranks among the shoddiest poems ever wished on us as the
product of genius! Its metre is difficult, granted. Yet with
faith in the power of inspiration to solve all problems of
craftsmanship, a poet may commit himself to a metrical
scheme that seems cripplingly tight and yet feel free as
air within it. Shelley, it seems, snatched idly at an idea
that entered his head one afternoon as he tried to locate a
lark singing in the sky, and began with:

Hail to thee, blithe Spirit!
   All unseen thou art,
That from Heaven, or near it,
   Pourest thy full heart
In happy strains of unpremeditated art.

In the golden lightning
   Of the setting sun,
Which the clouds is brightening,
   Thou dost float and run. . . .

Shelley goes home, fetches pencil and notebook, and jots down this much; but then discovers that he has rhymed *thou art* with *unpremeditated art*—which is a 'French rhyme' disallowed to English poets since Chaucer's time. One of the two *arts* must be struck out. So, having decided that the metre cannot be managed without recourse to near-rhymes like *wrought* and *not*; *spirit* and *near it*; *chant*, *vaunt* and *want*; he pencils the rhyme scheme in the margin, and changes his original *All unseen thou art* to *Bird thou never wert*, a dramatic statement irreconcilable with his later suggestion that the cock-lark's song is prompted by love for his hen. Nevertheless, he reserves *Unseen thou art* and *happy strain* for a subsequent verse.

A second difficulty is the golden light*ning* of the sett*ing* sun brighten*ing* the clouds. . . . Too many *ings*! He toys with his pencil, scratches his head, peels a grape, eats it, looks out of the window at the sun, and sees that it has sunk almost below the horizon. So *sunken sun*, instead of *setting sun*, gets rid of one *ing*; but he has forgotten that, unlike nightingales, larks never sing in a darkened sky, and that clouds never brighten, once the sun has disappeared, but turn a dingy red. No matter! The stars are coming out one by one, and it occurs to him that though an hour or two ago the lark was invisible even by broad daylight, neither could he see a single star. So, vaguely remembering the Psalm about the morning stars that sing together, and the Sons of God who shout for joy, he conflates the lark with the star into a single blithe Spirit springing like a fiery cloud higher and higher, while the pale purple evening melts around it, like a poet hidden in the light of thought. . . . This confused image has been much admired; but true poetic ecstasy makes sense, and more than sense.

The rhymes *higher*, *fire*; *springest*, *wingest*, *singest*; *Heaven*, *even*; *hidden*, *bidden*, are borrowings from the

Hymnal, and not long before his death Shelley thought seriously of becoming an Anglican clergyman. Here he pictures the poet as an amateur hymnologist: singing hymns unbidden. . . . There is something, I own, that endears Shelley to us—a generous-hearted muddle; the patent clumsiness of *To A Skylark* makes us feel for him as for a child of ten who has painted a sunset picture, thinks it wonderful and wants to be praised. We paste it into the family scrap-book and he signs his name to it in large, round characters. 'Nice fellow,' we say, years later, 'good Classic, went to Eton and Oxford, turned out neat translations from the Greek dramatists. Wouldn't hurt a fly; a bit of a radical, of course. Sent down from University for atheism. Pity! Deucedly odd at times—believe it or not, he used to put revolutionary broadsheets into empty wine bottles and throw them into the Bristol Channel, hoping that they might float across to Ireland! Wrote a sonnet about 'em too, beginning:

> Vessels of heavenly medicine, may the breeze
> Auspicious waft your dark green forms to shore
> Safe may ye stem the wide surrounding roar
> Of the wild whirlwinds and the raging seas—
> And oh, if Liberty e'er deigned to stoop
> From yonder lowly throne her crownless brow,
> Sure, she will breathe around your emerald group
> The fairest breezes of the West that blow. . . .

Sure, he got the colour right: Erin's own emerald. But why did he call for westerly breezes instead of easterly ones? Poetic licence, perhaps. Got drowned sailing in the Mediterranean. Sad, but hardly surprising!'

*

By way of contrast, a glorious example of how inspiration can make light of severe metrical discipline is Bernard de

TECHNIQUE IN POETRY

Cluny's twelfth-century *De Contemptu Mundi*, from which J. M. Neale translated *Jerusalem the Golden, with Milk and Honey Blessed*:

> Urbs Syon aurea, Patria lactea, cive decora,
> Omne cor obruis, omnibus obstruis et cor et ora.
> Nescio, nescio, quae jubilatio, lux tibi qualis,
> Quam socialia gaudia, gloria quam specialis.
> Stant Syon atria conjubilantia, martyre plena,
> Cive micantia, Principe stantia, luce serena. . .

Technically, the metre is called *Leonini cristati trilices dactylia*, and Bernard (who was an Englishman, though born in Brittany) has told how, though the Holy Spirit often begged him to write verses, he would not listen until the sudden cry came: 'Open the door to thy Beloved!' Then Bernard gave way, praying for heavenly grace that he might worthily sing his Beloved's praises. 'Open thy mouth,' he heard again, and felt inspiration breathed into him. Bernard writes:

And I say in no wise arrogantly, but with all humility and therefore boldness: that unless the Spirit of wisdom and understanding had been with me, and flowed in upon so difficult a metre, I could never have composed so long a work. . . .

Indeed, the *Contemptu Mundi* runs for some three hundred lines without flagging. We need not question Bernard's testimony that he wrote in an ecstatic love trance. There can be no other explanation. If only Shelley had written *To A Skylark* under the same spell. . . .

*

The Classical convention in English poetry broke down just before the First World War, and all subsequent attempts to reinstate it failed. Our modernists are still in

83

desperate search for a new convention of equal nonsensicality, yet of international prestige, which will create the impression that they are poets 'hidden in the mystic light of thought'. But what *objects* are the fountains of their doleful strain? Apparently the sole object is *technique*: which they have made almost a dirty word.

The Poet in a Valley of
Dry Bones

Granted a genuine sense of vocation, what technical advice can a young poet be offered? I dislike the word 'technique'. One hears: 'Yes, he (or she) doesn't *move* me in the least, but ah! what dazzling technique!' This implies intellectual achievement in any near-magical art or craft from which the intellect should, I believe, be barred for truth's sake, except as an occasional consultant on simple fact. Very well, then: what advice on craftsmanship, even if craftsmanship now means something quaint, laborious and out-of-date? But advice is what everybody gives and nobody takes.

As a young poet, I wrote my first serious poem in the summer of 1906, when I was eleven years old. I had been turned out of the family wagonette by my short-tempered grandfather, for having climbed aboard without my school cap; and so missed a picnic beside the river. I spent the afternoon working out a country-poem in rhymed couplets about a farmer who, so far as I recall, prudently harvested and carted his wheat just before a hailstorm flattened the crops of all his less industrious neighbours. The poem ended:

> The swain gave thanks at daybreak for God's grace;
> At Kirk this morn I saw his smiling face.

I remember thinking that *swain* and *kirk* and *morn* were very elegant words; and that I had scored off my grandfather (to whom, on his return, I dedicated the poem) by showing how little I cared for family picnics. This was a false start. Three years later I felt a genuine afflatus, and wrote one moonlit night in June:

O, not for me the lute or lyre!
A knight, I ride my thoughts of fire
And fly on wings for ever and aye
Through an unresisting starry sky,
Where the gleaming aether turns and sings
Its strange slow song of the birth of things.

There was a difference in kind between these two failures: the first, an academic exercise, was sadly deficient in technique; the second, a personal statement, was equally deficient in craftsmanship—but my hand trembled as I wrote it down; nor did I parade it for public approval.

One often meets a musical prodigy, but never a poetic prodigy, of tender age. A long, long experience with language is needed before words can fully collaborate with one another under the poetic trance. It seems necessary, too, to have read a great many poems by other writers, good and bad, before a poet can realize his powers and limitations. I never have much use for one whose poems I do not recognize at a glance as inimitably his own; even so, I reject them if they draw attention to a cultivated eccentricity, to pride in scholarship, or to the mastery of Classical or Modernist technique.

Shakespeare's plays can be arranged in chronological order, and the development of his verse-craftsmanship studied; but I am not a play-goer, and the comparatively rare occasions when he included poems in his theatrical declamations are all that really interest me. Some plays contain no more than a couple of lines; in others there are scenes consisting of poem sequences strung together on a thread of dramatic dialogue. Popular conventions were as strong in Shakespeare's day as now, and he could not afford to disregard them. No poet ever escapes from the epoch into which he is born; he can only transcend conventions by showing where they do not apply to him. And he should have a sense of belonging to a long line of former free spirits, and decide whether their divergences from contemporary fashion merit his approval; Shakespeare, despite his limited schooling, seems to have been fantastically well read.

The history of English poetry is traced in the text books as a succession of movements or schools—the School of Chaucer, the Allegorical School, the early Tudor Dramatists, the Euphuists, and so on, past the Anti-Jacobins, the Lake School, the mid-Victorian Romantics, etc., until one reaches the Georgians, the Imagists, and the Modernist Movement. But schools and movements are fictions. If a school, meaning the disciples and imitators of a particular verse-craftsman, achieves fashionable renown, this is a grave criticism of his sincerity. A poet should be inimitable. When two genuine poets recognize each other as true to their common vocation, this will only accentuate the difference between them in rhythm, diction and the rest. Any talk of a 'school' means that someone is peddling a new technique of verbal conjuring; as in commercial schools that teach writers of advertising copy how to make an easily hypnotizable public buy what they themselves must never believe in.

Craftsmanship is self-taught. A poet lives with his own language, continually instructing himself in the origin, histories, pronunciation, and peculiar usages of words, together with their latent powers, and the exact shades of distinction between what Roget's *Thesaurus* calls 'synonyms'—but are there such things? English has no officially approved way of expressing every conceivable thought, as French has; only precedents. A poet may make his own precedents, in disregard of any law of correctness laid down by grammarians—so long as they accord with the natural genius of English. . . . I studied French, Latin and Greek grammar at school, back in the reign of King Edward the Peacemaker, but was told: 'Only foreign languages have grammar', and expected to be treated as an imbecile or a yokel if I spoke or wrote bad

English. Its proper use was held to be a matter of good manners, not of grammatic law: I still hold this to be so.

Only wide reading, a retentive ear for conversation, and continuous dwelling upon words as disembodied spirits rather than as building materials, can equip a poet for his task. And what does 'equip' mean? It comes from the medieval Latin *eschipare*, 'to man a ship'; but had become metaphorical even before reaching England— Cardinal Wolsey uses it, first, in the sense of finding soldiers the necessary arms and accoutrements for battle. The poet should be aware, however, that the word *ship* is still latent in *equip*, and so is the sense of making ready for a voyage. In a true poem, produced by the deep trance that integrates all the memories of the mind, the dormant powers of each word awake and combine with those of every other, building up a tremendous head of power. How far the reader is conscious of the inter-related sounds and meanings depends on how much of a poet he, or she, is: for I allow the title of poet to all who think poetically, whether writers or not.

A historical dictionary should always be within a poet's reach: preferably the big *Oxford English Dictionary*—the two-volume edition is insufficient. Over thirty years ago, when I could not afford a set, I remembered the New Testament parable of the pearl, sold all my non-essential books, and bought it. I still consult the O.E.D. at least four or five times a day: never letting a doubtful word go by—I need to know its derivation, its first occurrence, its change of meaning down the centuries, and the sort of people who used it in different contexts.

*

The Vienna school of psychology presumes a conscious and unconscious mind as two separate and usually warring entities; but a poet cannot accept this. In the poetic trance, he has access not only to the primitive emotions and thoughts which lie stored in his childhood memory, but to all his subsequent experiences—emotional and intellectual; including a wide knowledge of English won by constant critical study. Words are filed away by their hundred thousand, not in alphabetic order but in related groups; and as soon as the trance seizes him, he can single out most of the ones he needs. Moreover, when the first heavily blotted draft has been copied out fairly before he goes to bed, and laid aside for reconsideration, he will read it the next morning as if it were written by another hand. Yet soon he is back in the trance, finds that his mind has been active while he was asleep on the problem of internal relations, and that he can substitute the exact right word for the stand-in with which he had to be content the night before.

One cannot hope to restore the creative processes that supplied certain unusual words in ancient poems. The work-sheets very rarely survive as evidence, and to discuss my own experience in writing poems suggests that I claim poetic merit for them: which no poet can afford to do. All poems are failures in the Muse's eye; and it is this conviction alone that entitles me to discuss the weaknesses in the work of others. One of the Muse's main functions is to abash her poet by making him aware of his stupidities, vanities, and petty dishonesties.

I once wrote a poem called *A Time of Waiting*, the theme of which was a resolve not to prejudice the future by hasty action:

> To take no rash decisions, enter into
> No random friendships, check the run-away tongue
> And fix my mind in a close pattern of doubt. . . .

When reviewing the second or third draft, I saw that *pattern* was too decorative a word.

> And fix my mind in a close *frame* of doubt. . . .

would have been too formal. I tried:

> And fix my mind in a close *net* of doubt. . . .

But a mind can hardly be fixed in a net; besides, *net* has the negative connotations of imprisonment without escape. I had in mind a positive form of quiet doubt, cultivated for the sake of good luck; because the Muse, for whose sake the doubt was assumed, would clearly not hasten to remove it. Finding the exact word seemed of the greatest importance: the poem, when complete, would confirm me in my decision. Poems have an auto-hypnotic function.

When I am writing prose and have a word on the tip of my tongue, or the nib of my pen, which somehow eludes me, I often consult Roget's *Thesaurus*. Reading the list of so-called synonyms in a word-group, I at once recognize the word I need. But I do not use Roget for poems. So, instead, on this occasion I went down to the sea, swam out to a small rocky island, and there the exact right word floated up to me from several fathoms down:

> To take no rash decisions, enter into
> No random friendships, check the run-away tongue
> And fix my mind in a close caul of doubt.

Caul surprised me, because I had not considered the word for at least twenty years; but later, reaching for the 'C' volume of the O.E.D., I found that it held all the senses I needed. A caul is, first, a net cap confining the glory of a woman, her hair; then a gossamer web spun by spiders over grass, heavy with dew at dawn. Finally, it is the smooth, cap-like membrane with which a child is sometimes born, a lucky relic of his uterine experiences and, in English superstition, sovereign against death by drowning. A caul is thus the gentlest and happiest of all cerebral restraints. I found three metaphorical uses of *caul*, which set a precedent for mine:

1579—Whoso is blinded with the caul of beauty. . . .

1636—Custom in sin had drawn a caul over my conscience.

1643—A caul drawn on the heart.

That *close call* has a somewhat outmoded slang significance, was an accident that did not disturb me. The eye cannot mistake *caul* for *call*, and the eye commands the inner ear. Poetry is read, not listened to, nine times out of ten. And *close* was the right adjective to qualify *caul*; I would have been ungrateful to look for another.

If a poem is lurking at the back of a poet's mind, and he has perfect confidence in bringing it to light under the trance, the key-words sooner or later will always fall into place. Or that is my own long-cherished superstition.

On the sole occasion that I ever discussed poetry with Walter De la Mare, I quoted him the lines from his *All That's Past*:

> —ah, no man knows
> Through what wild centuries
> Roves back the rose. . . .

and asked whether he was satisfied with *roves*. He blushed slightly, and admitted that though *roves* was too close in sound to *rose*, it was the nearest he could get—no, he wasn't satisfied. He needed some word that had the sense of *rambling*—as roses ramble—he had tried *Twines back the rose*, but *wild* and *twines* made an ugly assonance:

> Through what wild centuries
> Twines back the rose. . . .

Gads back the rose had a precedent in Milton's *gadding vine*, but *gad* was too similar in sound to *back* and, since Milton's days, had acquired a vulgar sense from *gad-about*.

De la Mare died without finding a satisfactory solution to the problem, perhaps because he was dealing with a conceit, not a poetic thought; and because the technical trick of metathesis—transferring the adjective *wild* from *rose* to *centuries*—had thrown the stanza out of gear. I have no hope of finding the exact right answer myself, because it was never my poem. I have tried ineffectually:

> —ah, no man knows
> From what lost centuries
> Wanders the rose. . . .

or:

> What old, dead centuries
> Bred the wild rose. . . .

But if it has to be *wild centuries*, then:

> Through what wild centuries
> Wends back the rose. . . .

is certainly better than *roves back*. *Wend*, a De-la-Mareish word, is akin to *wander* and *winding*, and makes a nice alliteration with *wild*.

The exact right word is sometimes missing from the dictionary. Thomas Hardy told me, in 1924 or so, that he now made it his practice to confirm doubtful words and that, a few days before, when looking up one such in the *Oxford English Dictionary*, he had found it, to be sure. But the only reference was: 'Thomas Hardy: *Far From the Madding Crowd*, 1874.'

I have myself hoped to contribute two or three words to the language. In a satire, *Beauty in Trouble*, I had occasion to mention the bat-like wings and cloven hooves of an evil angel. But *bat-like* is a plain, guileless Anglo-Saxon word, and the context demanded a rather grandiloquent Romance one to barb the satire. *Cat-like* and *feline*; *dog-like* and *canine*; *horse-like* and *equine*: these pairs, although synonyms for Roget, lie worlds apart. One sees the difference best in the phrase 'dog-like devotion'. 'Canine devotion' is not stubborn personal love but mere animal behaviourism. Very well: *bat-like* needs an equivalent formed from the Latin—as *feline* is from *felis*, *canine* from *canis*, *equine* from *equus*. . . . The Latin for *bat* is *vespertilio*; so I coined the word *vespertilian*—*vespertilionian* seemed too much of a mouthful:

> The fiend who beats, betrays and sponges on her,
>   Persuades her, white is black,
> Flaunts vespertilian wing and cloven hoof
> And soon will fetch her back. . . .

Among the gaps in the *Oxford English Dictionary* is *garden*: a jeweller's term for the bright cloudiness in certain gems, caused by chemical impurities, but giving them individuality and character. I am told that such a *garden* now proves that it is a genuine stone: the chemists who can artificially produce genuine rubies, emeralds, sapphires and the rest, have not yet got round to making any but flawlessly translucent ones:

> The pale rose-amethyst on her breast
>   Has such a garden in it
> Your eye could trespass there for hours
>   And wonder, and be lost.

Last year, I addressed the American Academy of Arts and Letters on the Arabic word *báraka*, which means the lively virtue, or blessedness, which a place or object acquires by long use; and deplored the new economic doctrine of built-in obsolescence, which sweeps away out-of-date models into the junk-yard or the garbage can long before they are worn out, and replaces them with others not meant to last for more than a short season. The lively virtue in words is longer-lasting. The doctrine of expendability applies either to semi-scientific terms which go out of date as the theses on which they rest are disproved; or to slang-coinages of novel terms for words like *money*, *liquor*, *girl*, *steal*, *cheat*, *policeman*, *fornicate*, *get drunk*, *die*, which add nothing to the simple original concept. A policeman is neither less nor more of a policeman when he is called a peeler, a bobby, an ecilop, a slop, a cop, a copper, a rozzer, a bull, or a fuzz. . . . Slang has been called 'poor man's poetry', perhaps because eighteenth-century Classical tradition insisted on a particularized poetic vocabulary; and so did the Romantic Revivalists, though preferring a 'Gothic' range of words borrowed from Chaucer, Spenser, Shakespeare, Walpole and Chatterton. Walter De la Mare is said to have started as a poet, while still a clerk with Standard Oil, by compiling lists of mellifluous words, such as *bergamot*, *chrysoprase*, *cresset*, *foredone*, *besprent*, and introducing them into nostalgic rhymes: his was a deliberate technique of quaintness.

The longer a word lasts in a language before growing obsolete—and one of a poet's moral duties is to rescue and reinstate obsolescent words for which no substitute can be found—the more strength and virtue it acquires. Yet there are well-dressed poems as well as naked ones, and the choice of vocabulary must always be directed by the theme. Donne, for example, specializes in the costumed poem, rather than the naked one. His *Seventh Elegy* alternates between the two different strands of language, Anglo-Saxon and Norman-French, rather than integrating them:

> *Nature's lay Ideot*, I taught thee to love,
> *And in that sophistrie, Oh, thou dost prove*

THE POET IN A VALLEY OF DRY BONES

> *Too subtile*: Foole, thou didst not understand
> *The mystique language* of the eye nor hand:
> Nor couldst thou judge *the difference of the aire*
> Of sighes, and say, this lies, *this sounds despaire*. . . .

He is working up to the grand close of five splendid
Romance words, introduced with eight Anglo-Saxon ones:

> I had not taught thee then the *Alphabet*
> *Of flowers, how they devisefully* being set
> And bound up, might with speechless *secrecie*
> *Deliver arrands mutely*, and *mutually*.

Donne gets away with a portentous word, *interinani-
mate*, in *The Ecstasy*, by using only Anglo-Saxon words to
introduce it:

> When love with one another so
> Interinanimates two souls. . . .

Shakespeare gets away in *Macbeth* with:

> . . . This hand will rather
> The multitudinous seas incarnadine. . . .

these being enormous, terrifying words suited to Lady
Macbeth's guilt and redeemed from bombast by the even
more terrifying simplicity of the Anglo-Saxon line that
follows:

> Making the green one red. . . .

To incarnadine and *to make red* are not, as is usually
thought, tautological; and though *to incarnadine* meant
only *to make carnation-coloured* like healthy cheeks,
Shakespeare was aware of its ultimate origin in the Latin
caro, carnis, 'flesh', and therefore of its association with

words like *carnifex* and *carnivorous*. He so aroused the latent meaning of murder in *incarnadine* that one cannot use it today without thinking of blood.

The lively virtue of words is something of which every poet must be aware. *England* has this virtue, and so has *Scotland*; but not *Britain*, which is an intellectual, not an emotional, concept. Nor has *Britons* much virtue, despite:

> Rule, Britannia! Britannia, rule the waves!
> Britons never, never, never shall be slaves. . . .

The adjective *British*, curiously enough, *has* acquired virtue because of the British Fleet, the British Grenadiers, and so on.

The exact rightness of words can be explained only in the context of a whole poem: each one being related rhythmically, emotionally, and semantically, to every other. This, in effect, rules out any use of the same word in different contexts, unless the two uses are consonant, or parallel. It also rules out any repetition of the same vowel sound, unless for some particular purpose, such as the deliberate stridency of repeated long *a* or *i*. Or as when Keats, who insisted on the need to vary vowel sounds in ordinary contexts, commends Shakespeare for writing of the bees:

> The *singing* masons *building* cells of wax. . . .

The four short *i*-sounds in *singing* and *building*, he said, suggested the low buzz of bees.

A poem always chooses its own metre, and any attempt to dress up an idea in a particular metre is, at best, an amusing parlour game; at worst, dreary literature. A poem begins with the usual line-and-a-half that unexpectedly forces itself on the entranced mind and establishes not only the metre, but its rhythmic treatment. . . . The basic English metre is the ten-syllabled iambic line. But the metrical rules, which in Latin poetry were always meticulously maintained, even though the context might be a passionate one, do not apply to English. A true iambic line in poems of emotional content has been rare since early Tudor times, and appears usually in lulls between gusts. The Earl of Surrey's proud requiem for his friend and companion-in-arms Thomas Clere begins, not in the measured iambic style, but with a drum beat:

> Norfolk sprung thee; Lambeth holds thee dead.
> Clere of the Count of Cleremont thou hight. . . .

before the iambic measure asserts itself:

> Within the womb of Ormond's race thou bred
> And saw'st thy cousin crownèd in thy sight. . . .

Shakespeare, in his indignant sonnet:

> Was it aúght tó mé, to béar the cánopy
> Wíth mý extérn, thíne oútward hónouring. . . .

does much the same thing. The rhythmic variations on this iambic line are infinite; yet, at the back of the mind, the metre still reigns.

The choice made by modernists of the nineteen-twenties to dispense with metre and rhyme altogether, because their Classically-minded predecessors had let these direct the poem, was unnecessary. Granted that a poet whose gentle voice rises and falls regularly in the iambic metre, with the expected rhyme closing each line, cannot hold my attention long. But whoever relies on what he calls 'cadence', as opposed to variations in metre, or changes the norm constantly without warning, cannot expect the Muse to approve, or the reader to follow him.

A young poet finds his greatest difficulty in ending a poem. The sudden occurrence of a poetic phrase and an idea are not enough: unless he recognizes that a complete poem is there, let him be patient. He has perhaps not yet learned how to integrate his whole mind in the necessary trance of attention. Donne is an extreme example of impatience: he often begins with splendid candour, and ends in crooked artifice.

When one treats poetry in this sort of way, the notion of technique falls away: all that remains is the poet's service to the Muse, his unwavering love of whom, for all her unpossessibility, assures that his work will be truthful. . . . Every dictionary is a valley of dry bones. The poet is inspired to breathe life into them (as Ezekiel did when he prophesied), and convert them into language. You remember the rattle and shaking, and how the bones came together into skeletons, every bone to its bone, and put on sinews and flesh. That is a metaphor of craftsmanship. Then the four winds blew upon them, and they stood up, in fighting companies; which is how poems come alive. Technique takes one no farther than articulating the skeletons with wire, and plumping them up with plastic limbs and organs.

Real Women

Ladies' Home Journal, 1964

Real Women

The most important historical study of all, utterly dwarfing all economic and political ones, is for me the changing relationship between men and women down the centuries —from prehistoric times to the present moral chaos in which both sexes have become equally confused about their roles. But I am a poet by calling, and have lived outside ordinary civilization for so many years that anything I write about real women must read oddly. Except perhaps to real women themselves, and the occasional man whom some accident of birth or experience tempts to agree with me.

A real woman, by my definition, neither despises nor worships men, but is proud not to have been born a man, does everything she can to avoid thinking or acting like one, knows the full extent of her powers, and feels free to reject all arbitrary man-made obligations. She is her own oracle of right and wrong, firmly believing in her five sound senses and intuitive sixth. Once a real woman has been warned by her nose that those apples are tasteless, or assured by her fingertips that this material is shoddy, no salesman in the world can persuade her to the contrary. Nor, once she has met some personage in private, and summed him up with a single keen glance as weak, vain or crooked, will his mounting public reputation convince her otherwise. She takes pleasure in the company of simple, happy, undemanding women; but seldom or never finds a friend worthy of her full confidence. Since she never settles for the second best in love, what most troubles her is the rareness of real men. Wherever she goes, her singularity will arouse strong feelings:

adulation, jealousy, resentment, but never pity for her loneliness. Real women are royal women; the words once had the same meaning. Democracy has no welcome for queens.

It would be wrong to identify the real woman with the typical wild one who, after a difficult childhood, has left home early to live by her wits at the expense of men. The wild woman is incapable either of friendship for other women, whom she cannot fail to regard as rivals, or of love for a man, her declared enemy. But at least she keeps her eyes open and ridicules the view that women must enthusiastically accept this glorious modern world of plenty bestowed on them by their hard-working menfolk, and that they enjoy being passionately swept off their feet and afterwards treated with amused indulgence. There was never, of course, any truth in the comic-strip legend of a primitive he-man who would grab his woman by the hair, threaten her with a knobbed club if she refused his advances, and haul her off panting ecstatically to his cave. In ancient Majorca, the island which I have made my home for more than thirty years, the woman, not the man, owned their cave; and, according to the Roman historian Strabo, if he took things too much for granted, she would merely say, 'Begone, and take your possessions with you,' and out he had to go—the children were hers in any case.

To reach some understanding of real women, one must think back to a primitive age, when men invariably treated women as the holier sex, since they alone perpetuated the race. Women were the sole agriculturists, guardians of springs, fruit trees, and the sacred hearth fire, and lived unaffected by any notions of progress. Tribal queens never thought in terms of historical time, but only of seasons; judged each case on its own merits, not by a legal code, as real women still do; and showed little regard for trade or mechanical invention. Chance discoveries or new techniques in arts and crafts were welcome, so long as these neither upset tribal economy nor enhanced the importance of individuals. It was the queen's task to restrain men from letting their ambition or intellectual curiosity override practical common sense, as it is still the woman's task to ask her husband: 'Must you kill yourself making money? Haven't we enough for the next five years at least, even if you stopped working altogether? Surely you don't enjoy your martyrdom?' But even if he cares to listen, social pressures compel him to provide for his family until he drops dead.

History begins with the emergence of men from female rule. They had at last discovered that a woman cannot conceive without male assistance—and brooded over the implications of this surprising fact. After long whispered conferences it was agreed that men ought to claim their freedom. They asked, 'Why should descent be reckoned in the female line, not the male? Why should a man when he marries go to the woman's home, not contrariwise? Why should a woman, not a man, sow the seed corn? Why should women control the tribe? Surely men are the true creators, sowers of seed, and therefore the holier sex, as well as being physically stronger?' Thus the male habit of reasoning from irrelevant facts, rather than relying on woman's practical wisdom, began the war between the sexes that has been raging ever since.

Men gradually usurped women's prerogatives in farming, magic, handicrafts, war—the Amazons are no mere figment—and government. The story is epitomized in a classical Greek myth: how the goddess Hera pitied a poor, bedraggled cuckoo and warmed him at her breast. This cuckoo was her brother Zeus in disguise, who ravished and humiliated her by seizing throne and sceptre. Later, when Hera and her kinsfolk rebelled against Zeus, he hung her from the vault of heaven, with an anvil tied to each foot. . . .

Men consolidated their victory. They reckoned descent in the male line, brought wives to their own homes, invented historical annals, legal codes, weights and measures, standing armies, engineering, logic and philosophy. On the excuse of protecting the weaker sex, they placed woman under male tutelage: henceforward she must serve her father's or husband's domestic needs as though not only spiritually but mentally inferior to him.

Greek myths record an occasional dramatic protest against this state of affairs: how the fifty Danaids stabbed their husbands, the sons of Aegyptus, on their common wedding night, and were punished in hell for this crime; how the Lemnian women murdered theirs for importing concubines from Thrace; how Amazons attacked Athens. . . . Yet, as a rule, the sex war has been fought sporadically in the home between father and daughter, husband and wife, mother-in-law and son-in-law. Only isolated regions, such as Galicia, Majorca and Pictish Scotland, kept their matriarchal traditions.

It seems puzzling that the real women of those days let all this happen to them. The sole reason I can suggest is that they thought far ahead. Since man had a certain undeveloped intellectual capacity, of which it would have been wrong to deny him full use, the real women sat back patiently, prepared to give him a free hand for some hundreds or thousands of years. Only a long series of disastrous experiments could make him realize the error of his headstrong ways. Eventually he must return to them in willing and chastened dependence.

Priests of the new male gods even modified the ancient myth of a sole goddess who had created the world, giving her a male assistant; and in *Genesis*—a comparatively late book—Jehovah creates the world entirely by Himself; and models Eve, the first woman, from man's rib! It is added that this woman's disobedience to God caused man to stumble and sin. In fact, the story is based on a

Hebrew pun: the same word means both 'rib' and 'make to stumble'. According to Hesiod's contemporary Greek myth, an inquisitive woman named Pandora opened a divine jar entrusted to her and let loose on mankind all the evils that now plague us. Yet 'Eve' was originally a title of the sole creatrix; as was also 'Pandora'.

Financial pressures of men's own making brought about the recent so-called emancipation of women. Grown daughters could no longer stay idling at home, a burden to their parents and to themselves until married off. Industry was booming and, with appropriate moral safeguards, they might fill the widening gaps in man-power. Women, who can now earn and keep their own money, even when wives, and have been granted the franchise—'franchise' originally meant 'freedom from being a serf'—need show men no gratitude for this liberality. Their freedom is still limited. They remain citizens of the second degree, auxiliary male personnel barred from all the highest offices; and would never have got where they are so quickly had it not been for two world wars and such loveless male inventions as machine guns, submarines, bombing planes and universal conscription.

Strangely enough, it is easier to be a real woman in backwaters of Christianity or Islam or Hinduism, where codes of behaviour have not changed for centuries, than in urbanized Europe or America. There she knows what part she must play, and can guard her inborn dignity. Although the husband, as head of the family, makes all decisions, he will never dare overrule even her unspoken protests. Among Majorcan peasants who live beyond the tourist range, no man would ever think of buying or selling so much as a hen without his wife's approval. She is always referred to as *la madonna*, titular guardian of the home.

What is home? In ancient days it meant a clan settlement, a camp or kraal, ruled by elders, where men had comrades and women their gossips, and children ran about in packs; and where a happy man-woman relationship could exist in some small corner away from the communal bustle.

Among us Westerners, because of man's jealous insistence on marital privacy, *home* has shrunk from settlement to farmhouse, thence to the cottage, thence to the 10-roomed apartment, thence to three rooms and a kitchenette with the usual labour-saving devices, in a huge residential block full of utter strangers. The housewife has her washing machine, telephone, television, refrigerator, electric cooker, car and door keys, to pay for which a husband must be out working all the week. She cannot regret (because she never knew) the easy companionship of her great-grandmother's day: quilting bees and husking bees, taking the cousins to do a week's washing down at the creek, lending a hand with the shearing and harvest, making jams and pickles, getting up round dances, singing and playing practical jokes. But no real woman can ever accept the present situation.

Man's logic has defeated itself. Boredom often drives the married woman back to a job as soon as she can leave her children at a nursery school; or to infidelity; or to an analyst. Home is home for only two days of the week. Which is why some paternally-minded industrialists take advice from professors of sociology and plant their employees all together in a wholesome suburban neighbourhood, where the company's standards of taste and respectability must rule their lives. Husband obeys boss; wife obeys husband, and preserves amicable relations with her fellow company wives, or else. . . . Spouses are thus shackled by a well-paid job to which the husband need no longer commute, by house, garden and swimming pool, by children, by hope of advancement and the prospect of a pension. Any sign of non-compliance is scored against both. No real woman can ever accept this situation either.

Attempts to liven things up socially are all too often masked under the dubious name of charity. It is characteristic of a real woman never to support public charities—on the ground that she neither knows the persons to whom her money goes nor has any assurance that it will be properly distributed. She gives only to those whose needs are familiar to her, and then from friendship, not pity. She will not be found at bridge clubs or at cocktail parties. Bridge, which is, after all, a money contest between individual players, cannot be a substitute for the good humour of a communal wash-day; nor can a cocktail party supply the intimate gossip of a quilting bee.

Wild women take advantage of this artificial state of affairs by exploiting the dormant dissatisfactions of husbands. One of them told me the other day, 'Yes, you may call me a mean, greedy, undependable, lazy, treacherous, spendthrift bitch. That's true enough a good part of the time; but it isn't the whole story. In fact, I've given myself to myself, and to no one else. My beauty is my own, and I take good care of it. If I choose a lover, I grant the lucky fellow no rights over me; and if he has sense, he won't claim any. As for breaking up a home, nobody can do that unless it's already cracked!'

A real woman likes beautiful things of her own choosing. She prefers a handleless cup, a backless chair, a mattress on the floor and a packing-case for the table to good taste conferred on her wholesale by interior decorators. There is an eighteenth-century English song, *Sally in Our Alley*:

> Her father, he sells cabbage nets
>   And through the streets doth cry 'em.
> Her mother, she sells laces long
>   To such as care to buy 'em—

Who'd think such rascals could beget
  So sweet a girl as Sally?
She is the darling of my heart
  And lives in our alley. . . .

The lover was a square: an honest, idealistic London apprentice, intent on becoming a journeyman, a master-craftsman and eventually a rich merchant—perhaps even Lord Mayor:

When Eastertide comes round again,
  Oh, then I'll have some money—
I'll save it up, and box and all
  I'll give it to my honey. . . .
And when my seven years' time is o'er
  Oh, then I'll marry Sally,
Ay, then we'll wed, and then we'll bed—
  But not in our alley!

Their broken-down, foul-smelling alley was a settlement, a home, the denizens of which were bound together by common poverty, shiftlessness, pugnacity, humour and a hatred of landlords and police. Yet no well-planned housing estate can ever compete with its spirit, which a Sally was always found to keep alive. From 1940 to '43 the German blitz levelled what remained of these alleys, and their sites are now occupied by large all-glass office blocks. The last of the Sallies found herself in a suburban life-box—one of hundreds built to the same design and set down in parallel rows—longing for a return to poverty, vice, dirt and even flying bombs.

Marriage, like money, is still with us; and, like money, progressively devalued. The ties between these two male inventions get closer and closer. Originally marriage meant the sale of a woman by one man to another; now most women sell themselves, though they may have no intention of delivering the goods listed in the bill of sale.

Not only is the wife, on an average, five years younger than her husband, but she lives statistically longer. So money power passes progressively into the hands of women. Also, divorce legislation (forced on guilt-ridden legislators by nagging spouses) grossly favours the wife. A youthful rival figures in most divorce suits, and though she and the wife seldom act collusively, they share an old-fashioned insistence on the honourable state of marriage, which enriches both. Wild women will commit matrimony when things go hard for them, without the least thought of keeping their obligations. The entranced husbands never know what has hit them, nor do they profit by the experience.

The United States, though often described as a matriarchy in all but name, remains patriarchal. Matriarchy, to be effective, needs real women. When women organize themselves intellectually on masculine lines, they merely stimulate the feminization of men, who, for terror of husband-hunting viragoes, are apt to seek refuge in the cul-de-sac of homosexuality.

Though men are more conventional than women and fear to infringe the Mosaic law (*Deuteronomy* xxii. 5) which forbids their wearing of women's clothes, women have no scruples about flouting the companion law: 'The woman shall not wear that which pertaineth unto a man . . . for all that do so are abomination unto the Lord. . . .' Even matrons now unblushingly wear blue jeans zipped in front.

The pseudo-patriarchal trend encourages women to respect legality, which they had hitherto found distasteful. A real woman, giving evidence in a court of law, scorns factual truth. Should her sense of equity run counter to the formal demands of justice, she will perjure herself in replies of cool and convincing honesty. When obliged to exercise a vote, she scorns the male axiom that the majority is always right.

A few real women survive in the old royal sense among West African queens, who rule with a silver knot-of-wisdom sceptre and claim the moon-goddess Ngame as their remote ancestress. A 'knot of wisdom'—known in English as 'the true lover's knot'—is the sort that tightens more securely the harder you tug at either end. Symbolically it means, 'My command can never be disobeyed!'

In civilized society royal women have neither thrones nor territorial queendoms, but the moon inspires them still, and they can wield formidable powers in times of emergency. Yet, since they avoid becoming public figures —the personality cult is another male invention—their names pass into history far more seldom than those of notorious wild women. A remarkable exception was Elizabeth I of England, whom her poets addressed as Cynthia—'The Moon'—and whose cynical disparagement of herself as 'but a weak woman' concealed an unshaken faith in her royal wisdom. Elizabeth ruled through awe and love, was on playful terms with her ladies-in-waiting, inspired her male subjects to feats of heroism and flights of poetry never known before or since among the English, always said 'No' to a doubtful petition and then slept on it.

A real woman's main concern is her beauty, which she cultivates for her own pleasure—not to ensnare men. Though she despises fashion as a male financial business, she will not make herself conspicuous by a defiance of conventions. The materials, colours and cut of her clothes, her hair style and her jewels are all chosen to match a sense of personal uniqueness. She can dress in advance of fashion, yet seem to lead it; and to any irregular features she may have, she lends a lovely ugliness denied to common beauty queens. Perfect detachment from the artificial or second-hand keeps her face unclouded. She has no small talk on current topics, and will suddenly vanish from a party, however grand, as soon as it grows boring.

If she plays games, it will be for fun, not competition; and if up against a win-at-all-costs opponent in tennis or golf, she will take care to lose handsomely—as one who competes only against herself. If she drinks, it will be because she likes the taste; and if she smokes, it will be for the same reason, not to steady her nerve.

She misses real men—men who would recognize her potentiality and agree that our world, despite its appearance of rational organization, is a wholly haphazard one, clanking on noisily to its fate along a random course once defined as 'progress'. And that a calamitous collapse must come before a new start can be made—from the point where the sex war was first declared and woman's conservative instinct as the guiding force of humankind repudiated. Because womanhood remains incomplete without a child, most real women marry—preferring simple, affectionate husbands who cannot understand them. This is not a renunciation of real love, since they agree with the thirteenth-century Countess of Narbonne: 'Conjugal affection has absolutely nothing in common with love. We say "absolutely", and with all consideration, that love cannot exist between husband and wife.'

Man's biological function is to do; woman's is to be. This difference is not a contrast of mere activity with mere passivity. 'To be' is indeed a full-time occupation. A real woman has no leisure in the modern economic sense —leisure as a consumer's relaxed insistence on commercial entertainment—but is always thinking, taking stock of herself, setting a stage on which actors can perform. If she paints or writes, this will be for her own private amusement, not to satisfy ambition; and if forced to earn her livelihood in this way, she repudiates the public personage forced on her by dealers and critics.

A real woman is content to dress with a difference, to make her home unmistakably her own, to illuminate any company she enters, to cook by instinct, not by the cookery book. This is her evidence of being, the proof of which lies in her sense of certitude. She is no feminist; feminism, like all 'isms', implies an intellectual approach to a subject; and reality can be understood only by transcending the intellect.

Mental institutions on both sides of the Atlantic house hundreds of young, beautiful, silently brooding girls, victims of the sex war—defeated before they could come to terms with life. Their tragedy has been brilliantly described in *The Ha-Ha*, a novel by Jennifer Dawson, whose heroine is almost a real woman, because: 'she never just plays a game with herself or other people, and refuses to learn the rules of society—meaning the worthy, useful, ordinary women who are so busy finding husbands and houses and good income brackets that they just haven't time to be conscious of themselves, and who see the world as an inventory, a container of so many things, and other people as so many tin-openers to undo it for them.'

The friendly and intelligent staff of the mental institution cannot persuade her that she should realign herself with the orderly outside male world. Being not quite real enough to escape defeat by pretending conformity, she loses all pride in her appearance, ceases to concentrate on any self-imposed task; and when at last she desperately breaks out, the police, we foresee, cannot fail to fetch her back for sedation and still closer surveillance.

A real woman somehow avoids suicide, or virtual suicide, or the mental institution; but is always painfully aware of having been born out of her true epoch; considered as either the past, or as the long-distant future. A sense of humour saves her from defeat. 'This is not worthy of me,' she will remind herself ten times a day, 'but to preserve my inner self I must once more act an alien part.'

None of her women neighbours, idly content with money and what it will buy, feel any need for drastic change in the man-woman relationship; she treats them politely, and has patience. If she ever comes across a real man, the thin thread of human hope that eventually the world will make practical sense again—cannot yet have snapped.

Moral Principles in Translation

Threlford Memorial Lecture, The Institute of Linguists,
London, December 10, 1962

Moral Principles in Translation

Though often having both translated, and been myself translated, I cannot claim to be a professional linguist: but at least to feel thoroughly at home in English; and to have picked up the main languages that formed it, more or less in the historic order of their appearance. That is to say I learnt, or rather absorbed, German as a child from my mother, whose family was Saxon; and from three long summer holidays spent on my grandfather's estate near Munich. Neither my accent nor my vocabulary has lost or gained much since I was eleven years old; and in conversation with Germans, idiomatic phrases float up unsought from the back of my mind. But I never learned to read the language in those days; so that now, if anyone writes me a German letter, I repeat the words aloud to myself and take them in through the ear. At Oxford, ten years later, Anglo-Saxon formed part of my English Literature course, and I found it easily understandable as a Germanic dialect.

French had been taught me at school by the hard way of irregular verbs and gender rhymes, such as *bijou, caillou, pou, chou, genou, hibou, joujou*; but at a period when we were on bad terms with France—the Entente Cordiale not having yet been cemented. The French master, an Englishman, although lavish with impositions if written work showed carelessness, never dared make us distort our mouths or lips for the correct pronunciation of *tu, du, pu, ému*, or *train, bain, métropolitain*, or *les feuilles d'automne*—he would have lost all control over the class. . . . I am still self-conscious about talking what Chaucer called 'French of Paris' as opposed to 'French

117

after the school of Stratford-atte-Bow'; and though my frequent visits to France, Belgium and Switzerland must add up to several years of residence, I seldom play the Parisian except over a telephone: for intelligibility. French remains a foreign language, not only because it was forced on me, but because I cannot think in the French way, and have a guilty sense of play-acting if drawn into complicated discussions with academicians or Left Bank intellectuals. Nor, apparently, can they think as I do, since fewer of my books have been translated into French than even into Hebrew, Finnish and Magyar. Nevertheless, I do feel at home with the language spoken by our Norman-French ancestors. Since they owned extensive domains in Southern France, it came close to the *langue d'oc*, or Provençal; and so does Mallorquin, the domestic language of Majorca, which has been my home for thirty-five years.

From the age of seven to nineteen I studied Latin, never rebelling against its discipline—perhaps because my father persuaded me that every gentleman must be a Latin scholar—and came to respect it as the most sober, economical and unambiguous of languages. Latin first made me conscious of the translation problem. German and English, even French and English, have close syntactical resemblances, but Latin taught me to think in a fascinatingly different way: with ablative absolutes, gerunds, and intricate Chinese boxes of clauses piling up to the resonant verbal finish. In the Latin Composition hour, each English sentence had to be recast Ciceronically. I can still write Latin hexameters or elegiac couplets on almost any subject at the drop of a hat; and (every second June) prepare a Latin oration, to be delivered at the Oxford *Encaenia*, in a sufficiently correct draft for two kind-hearted classical dons to polish. . . . Mr Charles Chaplin, who was being awarded an honorary doctorate on the 1961 occasion, told me afterwards how deeply he regretted never having had Latin included in his rough East End schooling. 'It is the backbone of English,' he said vehemently. And, indeed, in early Saxon times Latin was our sole literary language, and taught King Alfred, who translated Boethius and Bede from it, the art of clear expression.

At school I also learned Greek: which is too extensive a language to read without a dictionary even by those who have won first-class honours in Classics at Oxford or Cambridge, which I never did; and demands taste as well as precision from its students. Not every important Greek writer—important in the sense of providing reliable historic information or neat philosophical theories—is a good writer of Greek. . . . Incidentally, attempts have been made to remove St James's *Epistle* from the New Testament canon—on the ground that he wrote rather too well. But St James was an educated Temple priest, not a Galilean fisherman or Syrian tentmaker, and Alexandrian Greek will have been his second language.

My early affection for Greek allows me to distinguish good writing from bad; and I am more aware of its poetic potentialities than of Castilian Spanish, which I have read daily since emigrating to Spain in 1929. It seems, that unless driven by circumstances to adopt the customs of a foreign nation and break all contact with one's own, none but a born mimic can achieve full command of its idioms after his early 'teens. Besides, Mallorquin is the domestic language of Majorca; Spanish the official.

So I am lucky to have been educated in the main linguistic components of English: Latin; Anglo-Saxon by way of German; Norman-French by way of Mallorquin and French; Greek (which provides most of our scientific vocabulary); and Spanish, from which we have borrowed more than from any other vernacular except French. My interest in English is both loyal and practical. Since the age of fifteen I have been dedicated to one sole pursuit: that of poetry. And the writing of English poetry demands that one should know the language in depth as well as in breadth. A poem's emotional force depends on the strength and virtue of its component words; and the longer a word has been turned over by countless tongues and pens, and smoothed with use, the more powerfully will it strike home. This metaphor is, I suppose, suggested by the Old Testament account of how Israel's leading poet, King David, when he went out to fight Goliath, chose smooth pebbles from the brook as sling bolts. . . . Notice that this stark sentence—*David when he went out to fight Goliath chose smooth pebbles from the brook as sling bolts*—owes nothing to Norman-French. 'Thought' is an Anglo-Saxon word; 'fancy' and 'imagination' are of Romance origin. The thoughtful depth of English seems to be mainly Anglo-Saxon; the imaginative breadth, Romance. But since the language has been constantly changing down the centuries, and at various social levels, a poet should know the history of each word he uses. So, to a lesser degree, should all translators.

For some years I earned my livelihood by writing historical novels. There are two different methods. One is to enliven a chunk of ancient history by making the characters speak and behave in modern style. The central event in an early-Tudor novel published a few years ago was the Field of the Cloth of Gold, at which the heroine, a maid of honour to King Henry, remarked brightly to her chivalrous hero: 'I do hate parties, darling, don't you?' This fancy-dress foolery started, I suppose, with Mark Twain's *A Yankee at the Court of King Arthur*. The alternative method is suddenly to be possessed by a ghost with a grievance against historians, to relive his life, and re-think his thoughts in the language that he himself used.

I wrote once:

> To bring the dead to life
> Is no great magic.
> Few are wholly dead:
> Blow on a dead man's embers
> And a live flame will start.
>
> Let his forgotten griefs be now,
> And now his withered hopes;
> Subdue your pen to his handwriting
> Until it prove as natural
> To sign his name as yours.
>
> Limp as he limped,
> Swear by the oaths he swore;
> If he wore black, affect the same;
> If he had gouty fingers,
> Be yours gouty too.
>
> Assemble tokens intimate of him—
> A seal, a cloak, a pen;
> Around these elements then build
> A home familiar to
> The greedy revenant.

The theme of my novel *Wife to Mr Milton* came suddenly with the realization that Milton was what we now call a 'trichomaniac' (meaning, that he had an obsession about hair—his own, and women's). This discovery gave me the key to his lamentable marriage with Marie Powell of Forest Hill, truly a ghost with a grievance. Yet to keep any hint of modern psychology or sociology from intruding, I wrote the book in pure mid-seventeenth-century style, avoiding all words of later occurrence than 1651, the year in which she died. The language had to vary greatly from character to charac-ter—Marie Powell's main associates being Royalists and rural; John Milton's Roundhead and urban. Worse, she wore a dark blue favour, he a light blue—miscegenation between the Senior Universities can be dangerous in the extreme. . . . Here is Marie, accompanied by her humour-less and ambitious poet, in London at the beginning of the Civil War:

One early morning I went out with my husband to the Artillery Garden, where he performed military exercises in a company of volunteers from his 'Ward' banded together by their common religious interest. He told me, as he went, that he was a pikeman, not a musketeer, and that pikes are more honourable arms than muskets, in respect not only of their antiquity, but also of the colours flying upon their heads; and because with them is the Captain's proper station, the musketeers being posted at the flanks. He himself, he said, stood in the most honourable post of any Gentleman of the Pike, namely in the hindmost rank of bringers-up, or Tergo-ductores, upon the right hand; which also had the advantage of security. Then with his sixteen-foot pike, which he carried with him, he showed me, as he went, the several postures of the pike—the trail, the port, the shoulder, the advance, the cheek—and discoursed upon the use of each posture, heedless of the jests of the citizens and the winks of their wives whom we passed in the street.

I also wrote two novels about Sergeant Roger Lamb, a self-educated Dubliner, who fought with the 9th and 23rd British Infantry regiments in the American War of Independence. His language had a totally different rhythm and flavour. Here he reports on events leading to the outbreak of war:

Tidings of the Port Act were received by the Bostonians with most extravagant tokens of resentment. The text of the Act was printed on mourning paper with a black border and cried about the streets as a 'Barbarous Murder'. The terms 'Whigs' and 'Tories', for want of better, lately being intro-duced into America (the former covering those who favoured the action of the Bostonians, and the latter those who condemned it as turbulent and unwarrantable), a regular persecution of the Tories throughout New England now began. These Tories were for the most part people of property and education, descendants of the first settlers; but their barns were burned, their cattle driven, their families insulted, their houses broken into, and they themselves forced either to quit or starve. 'A Tory,' the Whigs held, 'is one whose head is in England, whose body is in America, and whose neck should be stretched.'

The most recent of my historical novels, *They Hanged My Saintly Billy*—Billy being Dr William Palmer, the poisoner, whose effigy I tried ineffectually to release from the Chamber of Horrors at Mme Tussaud's Wax Works— was written in the newspaper style of the 1850s and contained a good deal of race-course and hospital slang.

Here is a report from a former medical student, an associate of Dr Palmer's:

'Tell me more,' he says, handing me an uncommonly good cigar and igniting it for me.

'Well,' I said, 'it's this way. My "chums", as they call themselves, are sad dogs; very sad dogs indeed—though what the significance of "sad" in this phrase may be, I'm sure I don't know. They are, in point of fact, confoundedly gay, so gay as to be perfect bores. The *summum bonum* of their happiness seems to consist in strolling along the Haymarket or Regent Street of an evening, clad in ruffianly overcoats, smoking foul black cigars, and peering under the bonnet of every poor little dressmaker or milliner making her solitary way home, wearied after a day's toil, and weighted down by a heavy oilskin-covered wicker basket. They call it a lark to ogle the unfortunate girls and put them out of countenance—I call it blackguardedly. Then, when the shops are closed, and they have refreshed themselves at some public-house bar with copious draughts of half-and-half, they call it a lark again to march arm-in-arm, four or five of them, down quiet streets and shouting "Lullaliety!" at the tops of their voices.'

This period-style comes easily enough to whoever soaks himself in the contemporary literature and impersonates the characters. But what sort of English should be put in the mouth of an ancient Greek or Roman? Here we reach a more difficult moral problem. In my two Claudius novels, I relied on extant specimens of Claudius's literary style: his Latin speech about the Aeduan franchise and his Greek letter to the Alexandrians; besides numerous conversational fragments quoted by Suetonius, Dio Cassius, Seneca and others. Suetonius records that Claudius wrote 'ineptly' rather than 'inelegantly': the easy Alexandrian Greek which he used for his historical works will have come more naturally to him than polished Ciceronian Latin. I tried to reproduce the effect:

My tutor I have already mentioned, Marcus Porcius Cato; who was, in his own estimation at least, a living embodiment of that ancient Roman virtue which his ancestors had one after the other shown. He was always boasting of his ancestors, as stupid people do who are aware that they have done nothing themselves to boast about. He boasted particularly of Cato the Censor, who of all characters in Roman history is to me perhaps the most hateful, as having persistently championed the cause of 'ancient virtue' and made it identical in the popular mind with churlishness, pedantry and harshness. I was made to read Cato the Censor's self-glorifying works as textbooks, and the account that he gave in one of them of his campaign in Spain, where he destroyed more towns than he had spent days in that country, rather disgusted me with his inhumanity than impressed me with his military skill or patriotism.

In my novel about Count Belisarius, the sixth-century A.D. Byzantine general, I had to think in a less conversational and inept but equally fluent Greek, modelled on Procopius, Agathias and other near-contemporary historians; and put into the mouth of Belisarius's secretary. This passage tells how Belisarius's wife Antonina, a former Circus actress, won the distinction of being the only woman in history ever to unfrock a Pope:

> The Pope Silverius himself came to my mistress secretly, and said to her—I was present—'Most Virtuous and Illustrious Daughter, perhaps you will be able to persuade the victorious Belisarius, your husband, to give over his unwise intentions. It seems that he is intending to stand a siege in our Holy Rome, which (though abundantly blessed by God) is the least defensible city in the world, and in twelve hundred years of its history has never successfully stood a long siege. Its circuit walls, as you can see, are twelve miles in length and rise from a level plain; it is without sufficient food for its many hundred thousands of souls, and cannot easily be provisioned from the sea—as Naples, for instance, could be. Since your forces are insufficient, why not return to Naples and leave us Romans in peace?'
>
> My mistress Antonina replied: 'Beloved of Christ, Most Holy and Eminent Silverius, fix your thoughts rather on the Heavenly City, and my husband and I will concern ourselves with this earthly one. Permit me to warn your Holiness that it is to your advantage not to meddle in our affairs.'

For *The Isles of Unwisdom*, a novel that describes an abortive Spanish expedition to the Solomon Islands in 1598, I based my style on an account written by the Chief Pilot, a Portuguese named Quiroz; and used an old-fashioned nautical English with sufficient Spanish flavour to remind the reader in what company he was sailing. After the Admiral's lamentable death his wife, Doña Ysabel, took personal command of the fleet:

> The savages were indeed remarkably white: and so closely resembled Spaniards in shape and feature that the Captain of Artillery felt shame that his wife should see them stark naked, and sent her below at once. 'If they were monkeys,' he said, 'or African negroes, it would be a different matter; but it is shameful even for a married woman to be confronted by such

indecent sights.' Doña Ysabel and her sister, however, hung
over the poop-rail and watched the scene below without even a
flutter of their eyelids. The men were of graceful build: tall,
muscular, clear-skinned, with good legs, slender fingers, the
best teeth that ever I saw, and long curly hair, some of it very
fair and arranged in fantastic coils and plaits. 'God's death!' I
heard the Colonel cry. 'If these are the men, their women
must be beautiful indeed!'

The main problem of translation into English, an
extraordinarily pliable language, will always be finding
the level of diction that comes closest to the original. I
have translated from five different languages, and consider French the simplest to handle because, even though
Frenchmen occasionally rebel against their strait-laced
academic style which hardened in the seventeenth
century, *plus ça change, plus c'est la même chose*. A
translator must let French take its own course: that is to
say, he must imagine the author harnessing our barbarous English to his own inveterate elegance of speech.
Here is a passage from my translation of George Sand's
Un Hiver à Majorque:

In the ruins of a monastery, two strangers met by the calm
light of the moon. One appeared to be in the prime of life; the
other, though bent beneath the weight of years, happened to
be the younger of the two. Their encounter made them both
tremble, for the night was dark, the road lonely, and the
Cathedral clock tolled the hour with slow and mournful
strokes.

The bent stranger spoke first. 'Whoever you may be, sir,'
he said, 'you have nothing to fear from a man so weak and
crushed as myself. You can take nothing from me, either. I am
poor and destitute.'

'Friend,' replied the other, 'my only enemies are those who
attack me and, like you, I am too poor to fear robbers.'

'Then, brother, why did you start so at my approach?'

'Because, like all artists, I am somewhat superstitious, and
mistook you for the ghost of one of those departed monks on

whose shattered graves we are now treading. And you, friend, why did my approach equally startle you?'

'Because, being very superstitious, like all monks, I took you for the ghost of one of my fellows, who once buried me alive in the grave beneath your feet.'

This Anglo-French makes, I hope, inoffensive sense. It would have been wrong to mix vintages by translating George Sand into the crisper English style of her near-contemporary Dickens, perhaps as follows:

Two strangers met by moonlight in the deserted ruins of a Spanish monastery, just as a cathedral clock began dismally tolling the hour. Both started back in alarm. The younger of the two, who seemed crushed by years of suffering, spoke first.

'I do not know who you are, sir, but you have nothing to fear from a poor broken creature like myself; or I from you, since I am not worth robbing. . . .' Etc., etc.

Other ventures in translation raised a new problem: namely, had I any right to disguise an author's foibles, follies and clumsinesses, or to omit a large part of his perhaps admirably sustained, but no longer endurable, rhetoric?

English translators, from King Alfred forward, have always felt free to deal how they please with their texts. John Skelton, in his early-sixteenth-century version of *Diodorus Siculus*, is a good example of this. He did not, as a matter of fact, translate Diodorus's own Greek, but only Poggio's Latin abridgement, which he then expanded for the pleasure of Henry VIII's courtiers. Here is a passage from Diodorus's Book iv, Chapter 17—translated by George Booth, three centuries later, in a fairly literal sense:

Then Hercules destroyed the wild beasts in the deserts, and made Africa so quiet and improvable, (which was before full of hurtful creatures), that every part was fit for tillage and planting of fruit-trees; the whole country productive of wine and oil. In short, he so improved Libya (which, by reason of the multitude of wild beasts, was before uninhabitable), that no country in the world afterwards exceeded it for fertility and richness of soil.

This is clumsy writing, but not clumsier than Diodorus's. If asked myself to translate the original for ordinary readers, I should (like Poggio) cut out repetitions and integrate the sense at half the length:

Hercules then freed Libya, deserts and all, of the wild beasts that overran it; thus reclaiming an immense acreage for farming and fruit growing. In fact, the country has since yielded more wine and oil than any other in the world.

Skelton's readers must have been extraordinarily relaxed; non-religious books in English were few, and time hung always heavy on their hands through the long winter evenings. He could turn Diodorus into courtly entertainment by amplifying him with rhetorical flourishes to twice his original length, and to five times mine:

But Hercules having pity on the miserable depopulation and lamentable destruction of so noble a country, devised the means for to deliver them of this mischief. He animated himself to pourvey a redress, and by reason of this prudent policy he utterly destroyed all the wild beasts aforesaid and saved the country from all danger of the wild beasts aforesaid. And so all the coast adjacent he set in quiet and made them convenable and commodious to be inhabited, in making the soil apt for to be sown with all manner of grain, to plant and graft all manner of trees bearing fruit, to order their vines and improve the ground with such economical feats of husbandry that the ground was encrassate and enfatted meetly for the fructuous increase of their oils. Thus Hercules destroyed all the wild beasts and worms and so enprospered the region of Libya, that it flourished in worldly felicity and prosperous wealth more than any other realm of our knowledge or experience.

The translator's first problem is: what exactly does the reader need? Is it the literal text, in as faithful an English rendering as possible; or is it something a little more readable? If he needs a literal text, then Booth's version preserves most of Diodorus's felicities and clumsinesses. If he wants mere factual information, laid out in good order for his hasty eye to catch, then give him my version. If he wants fantastic chimney-corner entertainment in a rush-strewn mediaeval hall, give him Skelton's.

When my own books are translated into foreign languages, I much prefer to have this done by someone who writes his mother tongue well—that is, someone who thinks clearly—than by an expert on English literature. The clear thinker may make minor errors of translation, but will seldom commit me to a crude, illogical or ludicrous statement. Suppose, for instance, that he were French and I had made Lord Vere de Vaux ride out to the chase on his favourite steed, a flea-bitten grey. . . . He would hesitate to render this *son cheval gris rongé de poux.* Recognizing that it must be an English idiom, he would consult a dictionary of decent size and find that *moucheté* describes a horse of that peculiar coat. I never mind my sentences being cut and, some years ago, had only amicable feelings for the Finnish translator of *Count Belisarius* who wrote: 'I propose to omit three chapters, the contents of which are familiar to every Finnish reader.' And I am grateful to my younger daughter who has just edited a speech of mine for delivery at the Madrid *Ateneo* and made the English jokes sound Spanish; or, if that proved impossible, provided her own.

I have translated Marcus Apuleius's *Golden Ass*. He wrote a very ornate North African Latin, parodying the extravagant Greek with which street-corner story-tellers of Miletus in Asia Minor used to impress their simple-minded audiences. William Adlington translated it into comparably extravagant Elizabethan English; and his version is still preferred by the *Loeb Classics* editors.

Sic infortunatissimae filiae miserrimus pater, suspectatis caelestibus odiis et irae superum metuens, dei Milesii vetus-tissimum percontatur oraculum et a tanto numine, precibus et victimis, ingratae virgini petit nuptias et maritum.

Whereupon the miserable father of this unfortunate daughter, suspecting that the gods and powers of heaven did envy her estate, went into the town called Miletus to receive the most ancient oracle of Apollo, where he made his prayers and offered sacrifice, and desired a husband for his neglected daughter.

Since the stories need no rhetorical stiffening, I have translated them for the general public in the plainest possible English:

Her poor father feared that the gods might be angry with him for allowing his subjects to make so much of her; he therefore went to the ancient oracle of Apollo at Miletus, and after the usual prayers and sacrifices, asked where he was to find a husband for a daughter whom nobody wanted to marry.

This translation had two curious sequels. The Austra-lian government pronounced it obscene, and banished its importation, unaware that Adlington's less intelligible version had been on sale in Australia for a hundred years, and that *The Golden Ass*, when first printed in the fifteenth century, had been edited by a Catholic bishop. Next, a Stockholm publisher bought the Swedish transla-tion rights.

MORAL PRINCIPLES IN TRANSLATION

As a rule, I translate authors for whom I feel a strong liking: Apuleius, Suetonius, or Homer.... Once, however, I rashly offered to translate Lucan's *Pharsalia*, and hated every minute of it. Lucan had written this as a poem; but when Robert Frost defined poetry as 'what gets lost in translation', he was not referring to literary epics where the poetry is lost before the writing begins. I found the task could be decently undertaken only in prose; even so, to disentangle Lucan's meaning from his rhetorical artifice was most wearisome. He often strained sense almost to breaking point, as when he wrote:

> . . . excepta quis morte potest? secreta tenebis
> litoris Euboici memorando condite busto,
> qua maris angustat fauces saxosa Carystos
> et, tumidis infesta colit quae numina Rhamnus,
> artatus rapido fervet qua gurgite pontus
> Euripusque trahit, cursum mutantibus undis,
> Chalcidicas puppes ad iniquam classibus Aulin.

This has been translated in *Bohn*:

> . . . The secret recesses of the Euboean shore thou shalt possess, buried in a memorable tomb, where rocky Carystos straitens the outlets of the sea, and where Rhamnus worships the deity hostile to the proud; where the sea boils, enclosed in its rapid tide, and the Euripus hurries along, with waves that change their course, the ships of Chalcis to Aulis, hostile to fleets.

'Thou' refers to one Appius Claudius, whom the Pythoness at Delphi had ironically advised to escape the Civil War by 'taking his solitary ease in Euboea, that haven of refuge'. The sense is:

> 'Appius, you are indeed fated to take your solitary ease in Euboea: by being buried in a sequestered but famous tomb near the quarries of Carystos. It will face across the narrow

sea towards the town of Rhamnus in Attica, sacred to Nemesis, the goddess who punishes human ambition. In between lie the so-called Hollows of Euboea, where the sea is disturbed by the rapid, constantly-shifting current from the Straits of Euripus: a current which sets the ships of Chalcis adrift and swings them across to Aulis in Boeotia—that fatal shore where long ago Agamemnon's ships assembled before sailing for Troy.'

Since this is what the passage means, surely it should be so rendered? Why let sentences remain obscure, just because a few Latinists may nod appreciatively at the references to Agamemnon's marshalling of his naval forces against Troy; to the Goddess Nemesis's temple at Rhamnus; and to the asbestos quarries of Carystos?

Footnotes distract the eye and should, whenever possible, be brought up into the text. Here another moral question arises: how far can one's readers be trusted to catch recondite allusions in a foreign language? What, for instance, is the English for *Monsieur de Paris l'aura?* Should one translate: 'Monsieur de Paris (**Footnote*: the Paris executioner) will have him'? Or should one avoid the footnote with 'He's heading for the guillotine'? Or with the more colloquial 'Jack Ketch will get him'—although Jack Ketch used the noose, not the blade? How far can one safely underestimate the general reader's general knowledge?

When translating Alarcón's *Niño de la Bola*, written in nineteenth-century Spain, I was doubtful whether to retain the entire text of this passionate novel, or cut at least thirty pages of sentimental rhetoric that add nothing to the story. I cut. When translating the *Iliad*, I omitted one or two post-Homeric interpolations that spoil the narrative: for instance, the later events at Patroclus's funeral games which had not been announced by Achilles's heralds, and are not eighth-century in mood. And I rearranged the *Catalogue of Ships* in easily understood groups, according to the peoples, cities and islands that sent contingents. Homer repeats certain formal phrases of which one tires after awhile:

So spake the white-armed Goddess Hera, and the Owl-eyed Goddess Athene disregarded it not. Thus Hera the Goddess Queen, daughter of Great Cronus, went her way. . . .

Once Hera has been established as the daughter of Cronus; and Athene as Zeus's virgin daughter, to whom the owl was sacred, why repeat this information? 'Athene took Hera's advice, and went away. . . .' is enough. And when Zeus calls Athene 'the Alalcolomenean', surely the uninstructed reader—which includes most Classicists—should be told that Zeus was teasing his daughter: that Athene resented having been placed under the tutorship of Alalcolomenes the Boeotian, if only because the Boeotians were notorious for dullwittedness?

Paradoxically, the more faithful a rendering, the less justice it does the *Iliad*. Here is a typical passage from Book vi of Professor Lattimore's unexceptionally professional version, written in broken-backed hexameters:

Bellerophontes went to Lykia in the blameless convoy
of the Gods; when he came to the running stream of Xanthos,
    and Lykia,
the lord of wide Lykia tendered him full-hearted honour.
Nine days he entertained him with sacrifice of nine oxen,
but afterwards when the rose fingers of the tenth dawn showed,
    then
he began to question him, and asked to be shown the symbols,
whatever he might be carrying from his son-in-law, Proitos.
Then after he had been given his son-in-law's wicked symbols
first he sent him away with orders to kill the Chimaira. . . .

In other words:

The Olympians brought Bellerophon safe to the mouth of the Lycian River Xanthus, where Iobates received him splendidly: the feasting lasted nine days, and every day they slaughtered a fresh ox. At dawn, on the tenth day, the time came for Iobates to inquire: 'My lord, what news do you bring from my esteemed son-in-law Proetus?' Bellerophon innocently produced the sealed package, and Iobates, having read the tablets, ordered him to kill the Chimaera.

'Blameless convoy of the gods' and 'Proitos's wicked symbols' mean little to modern readers; nor will they recognize 'Bellerophontes' as 'Bellerophon', or 'Proitos' as 'Proetus', or 'Lykia' as 'Lycia', or 'Chimaira' as 'Chimaera'. . . .

Professor Lattimore is at least a scholar; far worse things are done in the name of translation by literary amateurs. Not so long ago, *The Times Literary Supplement* applauded 'the breath-taking magnificence and brilliant paraphrases of Ezra Pound's translation of Propertius'. He was said to be 'deliberately distorting the strict sense in order to bring out vividly Propertius's latent irony, and to have written what must surely prove to be a durable addition to, and influence upon, original poetry in the English language of this century'. Very well; I looked up two of the couplets quoted by the reviewer:

> Multi, Roma, tuas laudes annalibus addent
> Qui finem imperii Bactra futura canent.
> Sed, quod pace legas, opus hoc de monte Sororum
> Detulit intacta pagina nostra via.

A word-by-word crib would run:

Multi, *Roma*, many men, O Rome, *addent*, shall add, *tuas laudes annalibus*, praises of thee to the annals, *qui canent*, and shall prophesy, *Bactra futura*, that Bactria shall form, *imperii finem*, thine imperial frontier [i.e. that the Parthian Empire shall be absorbed], *sed*, but, *pagina nostra*, my page, *detulit*, has brought down, *hoc opus*, this work, *de monte Sororum*, from the mountain of the Sisters [i.e. the Muses of Parnassus], *via intacta*, by an untrodden path, *quod legas pace*, for thee to read in time of peace. . . .

Mr Pound's translation depends on an almost perfect ignorance of Latin, and a guessing at Propertius's sense from the nearest English verbal equivalents. As one might translate a dramatic account of Louis XVI's execution with: '*A bas la Tyrannie*', 'A stocking is tyranny', *s'écria Marat*, cried Marat to himself. *Le peuple, ému*, the purple emu, *répondit*, laid another egg. As here:

Multi tuas laudes, many of your praises, *Roma*, O Rome, *addent annalibus*, will be added by annalists, *qui*, who, *Bactra futura*, being Bactrians of the future, *canent*, will sing, *fines imperii*, about your fine empire. *Sed*, but, *quod*, what about, *legas*, reading matter, *pace hoc opus*, when all this work is at peace? *via*, a few, *intacta pagina*, unsullied pages, *detulit*, brought down, *de monte Sororum*, from the hill of Soritis [a word which means 'a forked complex of logical sophisms'].

Mr Pound has dressed this up as:

Annalists will continue to record Roman reputations.
Celebrities from the Trans-Caucasus will belaud Roman celebrities
And expound the distensions of Empire,
But for something to read in normal circumstances?
For a few pages brought down from the forked hill unsullied?

The book was advertised recently, with 'Except for a few pedants like Robert Graves, this translation . . .' etc.

I undertook to translate Terence's *Comedies* three years ago, but found his Latin so pure and terse that a faithful rendering would have been too dull for the stage. Yet the formality of the plot, and the most un-English atmosphere ruled out the use of modern slang. Luckily I came across a translation done in 1689, with fascinating vigour, by Lawrence Echard, a Cambridge undergraduate who later became Prebendary of Lincoln Cathedral; and realized at once that Terence's plays were vastly more readable when dressed up in the language of Restoration comedy. Echard wrote that Terence's bluntness of speech did not suit the gallant manners of his own times, but that he had taken it upon himself to correct this fault and, in some places, had lent the scene greater humour than it originally contained, though always keeping a close eye on Terence's design.

Here is my own attempted version of a scene:

BACCHIS, *entering, to her maid*: It's not for nothing that Laches has arranged this interview, and I'm pretty sure that I can guess what it's about.

LACHES, *aside*: I must see that my anger doesn't prevent me from persuading her to do as I wish; or make me act in a way I might afterwards regret. I'll go up to her. Good day, Bacchis!

BACCHIS: Good day, Laches. . . .

LACHES: I have no doubt that you wonder why I sent for you?

BACCHIS: Yes, I am a little timid when I consider what I am, lest your knowledge of my trade might be to my disadvantage; but I can easily defend my moral character. . . .

And this is Echard's version:

BACCHIS, *entering*: I'll be sworn 'tis no small matter that makes Mr Laches send to speak with me now. Yet, in truth, I'm mightily mistaken if I don't guess what the business is.

LACHES, *to himself*: I must take special care that my passion neither hinders me from bending her to my wishes, nor makes me do in haste what I may repent at leisure. . . . I'll accost her. . . . Mrs Bacchis, your servant!

BACCHIS: Yours, good Mr Laches.

LACHES: Truth, I don't doubt but what you somewhat wonder why I sent to speak with ye.

BACCHIS: And really when I consider that question myself, I
fear lest the scandal of my trade should prejudice you
against me. For, as to my honest behaviour in it, I defy the
world to accuse me. . . .

It will easily be seen how much better than mine
Echard's level of English suits Terence.

Daring essays in the translation of Aristophanes have
recently been made by a group of American writers. I do
not dislike attempts at modernizing ancient dramas, such
as Jerome Robbins's *West Side Story*, which plainly
depends on *Romeo and Juliet*; but I think it unfair to
father sophisticated New World obscenities on Aristophanes not even hinted at in his text.

Mr William Arrowsmith justifies a new version of
The Birds as follows:

Rhetorical conventions and jargon. What is true of dialects is
also true of professional rhetoric and jargon: if they are to be
comic, they have to be translated into an apposite convention
of English rhetoric or jargon. Invariably, this means that their
language must be heightened and made even more ponderous
than it is in the Greek. The astronomer Meton, for instance, is
used by Aristophanes to parody the jargon and abstruse pom-
posity of sophistic science. But because Greek scientific jargon
was a relatively immature growth (at least when compared
with the jargons of modern science), his words, literally
translated, sound to modern ears merely somewhat silly. In the
circumstances, I deliberately heightened this language, adding
technical terms and jargonizing it further, in the belief that
only by so doing could I create the effect of gobbledegook that
Meton's demonstration was intended to have for Athenian ears.

Here is Mr Arrowsmith's handling of the theme:

PISTHETAIROS: And those tools?
METON: Celestial rules, of course.
Now attend, sir.
Taken *in extenso*,

our welkin resembles a cosmical charcoal oven or potbellied stove worked by the convection principle, though vaster. Now then, with the flue as my base, and twirling the calipers thus, I obtain the azimuth, whence, by calibrating the arc or radial sine—you follow me, friend?

PISTHETAIROS: No, I don't follow you.

METON: No matter. Now then, by training the theodolite here on the vector's zenith tangent to the Apex A, I deftly square the circle, whose conflux, or C, I designate as the centre or axial hub of Cloudcuckooland, whence, like global spokes or astral radii, broad boulevards diverge centrifugally, forming, as it were. . . .

At this point in translation, I think, one should adopt the Victorian descriptive phrase: '*After Aristophanes*'.

To sum up. A translator's first duty must always be to choose the appropriate level of his own language for any particular task.

His second duty is to beware of a deceptive resemblance between words in allied languages. For example, in Spanish *actual* means 'contemporary'; *justificación* may mean 'an apology'; *barba*, a woman's or a child's chin; and a *biftec* is as likely to be pork or lamb as beef. *Lechería* is a 'dairy', not a brothel. The French for 'encore' at a theatre is *bis*. . . .

His third duty will be to treat the other man's work with as much respect as if it were his own, and present it with loving care—which means, in practice, correcting small faults and clarifying references. But, though entitled to abridge when boredom threatens, he must never foist new ideas on the original.

Finally he must realize that translation is a polite lie, but nevertheless a lie. . . . *Ein Stückchen Brot, un morceau de pain, un trozito de pan*, are all similarly rendered in English as 'a morsel of bread'. But the altogether different sounds of these words convey immense variations in shape, colour, size, weight and taste of the breadstuff to which they refer, and in the eater's attitude to them.

Perhaps my linguistic shortcomings have tempted me to over-emphasize the importance of knowing one's own language. You may recall the famous conversation—preserved, I think, by Charles Lever—between a musketeer of the Irish Brigade that fought at Fontenoy, and a French sentry:

> Qui va là? *says he.*
> Je, *says I, knowing their lingo.*
> Où est votre lanterne? *says he.*
> Mon lantern a sorti, *says I.*
> Comment? *says he.*
> Come on, then, *says I; and with that I struck him.*

Intimations of the Black Goddess

Combining three Oxford Lectures,
Michaelmas Term, 1963

Intimations of the Black Goddess

Poets, like prophets and saints, claim to live by certain unshakeable principles. But just as the sole judge of saintliness or prophetic truth is God—not popular awe or fallible Church Councils; so the sole judge of poetry for the professed poet, is the Muse-goddess—not textbook critics or auditors of publishers' net-sales. Her inspiration has from time to time been manifested, or presumed, in poems; like that of God in prophecies. But since neither deity ever issues an authentic Royal warrant for any particular servitor, prophets have often prophesied erroneously in God's name; and poets have often misrepresented the Muse.

Though able to prove myself a former soldier by producing a row of tarnished campaign medals, I cannot show that I am a poet merely by displaying a row of well-thumbed verse-volumes. No public honours, no consensus of other poets, no album of press-cuttings, nor even the passage of time itself can give me, or anyone else, more than the courtesy title of poet. The one sure reward for whatever labours we may have undergone is our continued love of the Muse: as prophets count on none other than their continued fear of God. Undeniably a prophet will feel reassured if, in answer to his prayer, he sees the tyrant humiliated, the leper cleansed, the shadow turned back on the sun-dial. Undeniably, too, the poet will feel reassured if, reading what he has written for the Muse's sake, he finds that by some miracle he has said almost exactly what he meant.

The inspired Hebrew prophets were at constant loggerheads not only with the endowed Levitic priesthood, but

143

with the monarchy, of which Samuel had always voiced his disapproval: calling for a pure theocracy. And God, it was agreed, chose prophets by certain signs known only to Himself; not they, God. The prophetic age ended for Israel early in the second century B.C., when her Guild of Prophets was disbanded by the Sanhedrin; as it likewise ended for orthodox Christians at the Crucifixion—when all prophecies were thought to have been fulfilled. Since then, the Jews acknowledge only sages—because prophets answer directly to God, but sages must refer to God's unalterable written Law. And the Church acknowledges only saints—always after strict inquiry into their orthodoxy. Catholic saints (there are, of course, no Protestant saints, with the dubious exception of King Charles the Martyr) live in the Church's shadow, accept her dogma and, because neither married nor forced to earn their livelihood, occupy their entire lives in prayer, preaching, vigils, fasting, and good works. Poets, on the other hand, like prophets, reject dogma and patronage as contravening freedom of thought, and take care to live outside the literary establishment in the rough-and-tumble lay world.

Hebrew prophets gave God sole credit for any miracles done through them; a poet gives the Muse sole credit for his poems. But God, for the prophets, was a national deity; the Muse, though originally a tribal goddess, must now be a personal one. Prophets, moreover, being recognized as holy men, could count on hospitality wherever they went, and therefore—as we learn from the story of Elijah and Naaman—refused all payment for their works; but poets cannot count on such generous treatment as they could in ancient Ireland, for times have changed. They view what they have written as the Muse's clarifications of their own confused thought; not as saleable products or passports to fame—lest they incur her deep displeasure. Nevertheless, if their poems receive public acclaim, they need not feel guilty, having meant them, first, for the

Muse's eye. When Shakespeare opened a sonnet with *'Devouring Time, blunt thou the lion's claws'*, and ended it: *'My love shall in my verse ever live young'*, he was thinking of the immortal fame thus conferred on his love, rather than of his own. Some poets affect to despise immediate fame, and address posterity—though with small reason to assume that posterity will be more perspicacious than their own turnip-headed fellow-citizens.

The chaotic ethics of our epoch derive, I believe, from a revolution in early historical times that upset the balance between male and female principles: namely, the supersession of matriarchy by patriarchy. This revolt, and the subsequent patriarchal cult of reason (as opposed to intuitive thought), gave men control over most domestic, agricultural, and other arts. Women became chattels, no longer able even to bestow their love freely or educate their own children.

The poetic trance derives from ecstatic worship of the age-old matriarchal Greek Muse, who ruled Sky, Earth, Underworld in triad, and was worshipped on mountains. Hence her name—the Greek word *mousa* being etymologically connected with the Latin *mons*. Her altars—stone herms, or baetyls, around which women devotees danced counter-sunwise at lunar festivals—stood on the foot-hills of Parnassus, Olympus and Helicon. A male dance-leader, originally her willing sacrificial victim, invoked the Muse by improvising hexameter verses to a lyre accompaniment that set an ecstatic round dance in motion. Presently the Muse—like the goddess Erzulie in Haitian *voudoun*—entered into, or 'rode', some woman dancer, who now acted, spoke and sang on her mistress's behalf. 'Sing, Muse!' had a literal meaning: it was a leader's appeal to the Goddess—'Choose your vessel, and sing to us through her mouth!'

At some time before the eighth century B.C., the god Apollo took over Muse-worship and, calling himself

'Leader of the Muses', transferred her cult to his own
sacred precincts. This meant more than self-identifica-
tion with the lyre-plucking dance-leader of a nine-woman
Maenad company; he was asserting his authority over
the Muse herself. The Homeric bards, who based their
guild on holy Delos, were Apollo's servitors, itinerant
ballad-singers—'ballads' being originally dance songs—
and claimed that they could induce the genuine Muse-
trance even in a mixed and sedentary audience.

Though, at a later date, ballads were often recited
without music, dance measures remained essential to
poetic composition: creating a strong hypnotic suggesti-
bility in listeners—and, when written down, in readers.
By this stage, however, the Muse's invocation had become a mere formality. Once her worship was separated
from the altar rites, she never again spoke through a
woman worshipper. Apollo, as Leader of the Muses,
henceforth dictated poems. 'Metres', originally dance
measures, were formalized by the Greek epic and dramatic poets, who applied to them strict Apollonian rules:
each variety of metrical foot being assigned its proper
emotional use. Yet Apollo, though the patron of formal
verse (which included literary epics, odes, hymns and
Classical idylls), was incapable of supplying the authentic
trance, and discouraged ecstatic utterances except from
his own highly tendentious oracles.

The basis of poetry is love, but love between men
(apart from rare homosexual pairs) is seldom more than a
metaphor—Christians preach on brotherly love, but look
how most brothers treat one another! Love between men
and women is a fundamental emotion, strong enough to
transcend social contracts; and the love bestowed on a
poet, however briefly, by a Muse-possessed woman,
heightens his creative powers to an unparalleled degree.
Poets demand inspiration, rather than tutoring in verse
technique by experts of their own sex.

The peculiar strength of the Muse lies in her need to bestow love freely and absolutely, without incurring the least contractual obligation: having chosen a poet, she dismisses him in favour of another, whenever she pleases and without warning. He must never count on her constancy, on her honour, or on her sympathy with his sufferings, but remain faithful beyond reason. And though deep in her heart she may respect nobody more than himself, he must not presume on this knowledge nor be deceived by her actions. The prophet's love of his God, a metaphor of filial reverence for a stern father, had this in common with poetic love—that the prophet was unable to count on God's attention to his prayers.

Poetry is a way of thought—non-intellectual, anti-decorative thought at that—rather than an art. Would-be poets today experiment in new loveless Apollonian techniques, taking pictorial abstractionism as their model, all working 'objectively'—that being for them a term of praise—and unprepared to accept the poetic trance with its fantastic co-ordination of sound, rhythm and meaning. Poets who serve the Muse wait for the inspired lightning flash of two or three words that initiate composition and dictate the rhythmic norm of their verse.

DANCE OF WORDS

To make them move, you should start from lightning
And not forecast the rhythm: rely on chance
Or so-called chance, for its bright emergence
Once lightning interpenetrates the dance.

Grant them their own traditional steps and postures
But see they dance it out again and again
Until only lightning is left to puzzle over—
The choreography plain, and the theme plain.

There are two distinct, but complementary, orders of women, both of them honoured by poets. First, the ideal woman of patriarchal civilization whom the Greeks deified as the Goddess Hestia, the Latins as Vesta; and who is represented in Christianity by the Virgin Mary—heroine of all old-fashioned songs and stories. Beautiful, tender, true, patient, practical, dependable: the woman whom Solomon described as 'more precious than rubies' —the guardian of the sacred hearth, the wife-to-be, dreamt of by romantic soldiers in desert bivouacs.

Then the other woman: the multitudinously named White Goddess, a relic of matriarchal civilization or (who knows?) the harbinger of its return. She scorns any claim on her person, or curb on her desires; rejects male tutelage, hates marriage, and demands utter trust and faithfulness from her lovers—treating love not as a matter of contract, but as a sudden, unforeseeable miracle. She punishes the pride of any suitor who dares hope that he will one day make her his wife. Here is a poem on the subject, cast in seventeenth-century ballad form:

INKIDOO AND THE QUEEN OF BABEL

When I was a callant, born far hence,
You first laid hands on my innocence,
But sent your champion into a boar
That my fair young body a-pieces tore.

When I was a lapwing, crowned with gold,
Your lust and liking for me you told,
But plucked my feathers and broke my wing—
Wherefore all summer for grief I sing.

When I was a lion of tawny fell,
You stroked my mane and you combed it well,
But pitfalls seven you dug for me
That from one or other I might not flee.

When I was a courser, proud and strong,
That like the wind would wallop along,
You bated my pride with spur and bit
And many a rod on my shoulder split.

148

INTIMATIONS OF THE BLACK GODDESS

When I was a shepherd that for your sake
The bread of love at my hearth would bake,
A ravening wolf did you make of me
To be thrust from home by my brothers three.

When I tended your father's orchard close
I brought you plum, pear, apple and rose,
But my lusty manhood away you stole
And changed me into a grovelling mole.

When I was simple, when I was fond,
Thrice and thrice did you wave your wand,
But now you vow to be leal and true
And softly ask, will I wed with you?

The original of these stanzas was written more than four thousand years ago—the hero Enkidu's address to the Love-goddess Ishtar. I have translated them word for word from the Babylonian *Gilgamesh Epic*, though omitting to name the 'callant born far hence'—in the original, he figured as 'Tammuz'; for the Greeks he was Adonis. Enkidu's refusal to trust Ishtar a seventh and last time, earned him the punishment of death without resurrection. It is from this order of wild women that the Muse always emerges. The melancholy strain in traditional poetry records the poet's disappointment that she cannot behave like Vesta.

Odes to the Vestal Virgin Mary have been written by Catholic poets since her sudden rise to power during the Crusades. None ever charges her with unkindness. Poets call on the Blessed Virgin to stand by them even in essentially male occupations. She will guide a battered barque safe to port; bless a young knight's sword after his all-night vigil, and direct it shrewdly when he takes the field; with a twitch of her blue mantle she will draw a murderous bull from the gored matador. . . . But her facial expression never varies, nor do her simple gestures. She offers no surprises, never jokes, teases, hides. Small furry animals gather around her. With lion, fox, lynx, hawk or osprey she has no dealings. She will watch at the sick-bed, drudge in the houses of the poor, wear the plainest clothes, and instruct the men of her household by example only, never by harsh words or deception. The difference between these complementary characters is presented in:

RUBY AND AMETHYST

Two women: one as good as bread,
  Bound to a sturdy husband.
Two women: one as rare as myrrh
  Bound only to herself.

Two women: one as good as bread,
  Faithful to every promise.
Two women: one as rare as myrrh,
  Who never pledges faith.

The one a flawless ruby wears
  But with such innocent pleasure
A stranger's eye might think it glass
  And take no closer look.

Two women: one as good as bread,
  The noblest of the city.
Two women: one as rare as myrrh,
  Who needs no public praise.

The pale rose-amethyst on her breast
  Has such a garden in it
Your eye could trespass there for hours,
  And wonder, and be lost.

About her head a swallow wheels
  Nor ever breaks the circuit:
Glory and awe of womanhood
  Still undeclared to man.

INTIMATIONS OF THE BLACK GODDESS

> Two women: one as good as bread,
>   Resistant to all weathers.
> Two women: one as rare as myrrh,
>   Her weather still her own.

The Muse and Vesta rule different worlds. Yet few rubies are unflawed. The sacred hearth fire is often left unattended, and to marry even the Virgin Mary herself did not make a poet of St Joseph. . . . In fact, more poems spring from a realization that domestic love has cooled or died than from resolute praises of domesticity; and the Muse, the perpetual Other Woman, always inspires them. Nevertheless, there are settled marriages over which the White Goddess has no power. She will smile if the husband writes his faithful wife a well-turned ode on their silver wedding anniversary, and pass on with a disdainful shrug.

On consulting the *Oxford English Dictionary*, to discover from its dated quotations what English poet had first written of an inspiratory Muse possessing a particular woman, I was surprised to find no such concept mentioned, though it has lately become a literary commonplace. Occasional women—such as the Mexican prodigy Juana de Asbaje—have indeed been hailed as 'The Tenth Muse'; but as poets themselves, not as patronesses or guardians of poets. . . . Though I have believed in a personal Muse for so long that I cannot recall her first entry into my heart, I would feel far happier to know that some other poet—Raleigh or Coleridge or Keats, for instance, all of whom record their visions of the Muse-goddess—had anticipated me in this usage.

Only during the past three years have I ventured to dramatize, truthfully and factually, the vicissitudes of a poet's dealings with the White Goddess, the Muse, the perpetual Other Woman. Whatever may be said against her, she at least gives him an honest warning of what to expect—as it were, tying a poison label around her own neck:

LYCEIA

All the wolves of the forest
Howl for Lyceia,
Crowding together
In a close circle,
Tongues a-loll.

A silver serpent
Coiled at her waist
And a quiver at knee,
She combs fine tresses
With a fine comb:

Wolf-like, woman-like,
Gazing about her,
Greeting the wolves;
Partial to many,
Yet masked in pride.

The young wolves snarl,
They snap at one another
Under the moon.
'Beasts, be reasonable,
My beauty is my own!'

Lyceia has a light foot
For a weaving walk.
Her archer muscles
Warn them how tightly
She can stretch the string.

I question Lyceia,
Whom I find posted
Under the pine trees
One early morning:
'What do the wolves learn?'

INTIMATIONS OF THE BLACK GODDESS

'They learn only envy,'
Lyceia answers,
'Envy and hope,
Hope and chagrin.
Would you howl too
In that wolfish circle?'
She laughs as she speaks.

The poet listens to her warning:

THE DANGEROUS GIFT

Were I to cut my hand
    On the sharp knife you gave me
    (That dangerous knife, your beauty),
I should know what to do:
    Bandage the wound myself
And hide the blood from you.

A murderous knife it is,
    As often you have warned me:
    And if I looked for pity
Or tried a wheedling note
    Either I must restore it
Or turn it on my throat.

The Muse shows a childish delight at being recognized
by her poet, and may at first profess grateful love, though
never giving him the least assurance of her continuous
accessibility:

SELDOM, YET NOW

Seldom, yet now: the quality
Of this fierce love between us—
Seldom the encounter,
The presence always,
Free of oath or promise.

And if we were not so,
But birds of similar plumage caged
In the peace of everyday,
Could we still conjure wildfire up
From common earth, as now?

Soon the Muse will multiply her evasions and broken promises, while still demanding the poet's absolute trust; take gifts as her right, rule him with a whim of iron, and subject him to almost insufferable ordeals. . . . If he remains faithful, she will choose a new lover from among his friends; as in the Anatha-Ishtar myth, she always betrayed and murdered him for the sake of his twin, the anti-poet:

HORIZON

On a clear day how thin the horizon
Drawn between sea and sky,
Between sea-love and sky-love;
And after sunset how debatable
Even for an honest eye.

'Do as you will tonight,'
Said she, and so he did
By moonlight, candlelight,
Candlelight and moonlight,
While pillowed clouds the horizon hid.

Knowing-not-knowing that such deeds must end
In a curse which lovers long past weeping for
Had heaped upon him: she would be gone one night
With his familiar friend,
Granting him leave her beauty to explore
By moonlight, candlelight,
Candlelight and moonlight.

Yet the Muse can exercise no power without her poet, and he is aware of this; but dares not disclose her dependence on his love. *Enkidu and the Queen of Babel* is to the point here:

> When I was a lion of tawny fell,
> You stroked my mane and you combed it well,
> But pitfalls seven you dug for me
> That from one or other I might not flee. . . .

Ishtar, Queen of Babylon, was the original Virgin of the Zodiac, who appears on steles, naked and riding a lion, the poet's zodiacal sign:

LION LOVER

> You chose a lion to be your lover—
> Me, who in joy such doom greeting
> Dared jealously undertake
> Cruel ordeals long foreseen and known,
> Springing a trap baited with flesh: my own.
>
> Nor would I now exchange this lion heart
> For a less furious other,
> Though by the Moon possessed
> I gnaw at dry bones in a lost lair
> And, when clouds cover her, roar my despair.
>
> Gratitude and affection I disdain
> As cheap in any market:
> Your naked feet upon my scarred shoulders, ·
> Your eyes naked with love,
> Are all the gifts my beasthood can approve.

Though the poet's friends may descry his Muse as a vixen, a bitch, a bird of prey, he is pledged to accept what he would refuse from any other woman; and suffers most when she uses the light of glory with which he invests her, to shine in an anti-poetic and even criminal world. Is she, in truth, his Muse, his love? Or is she acting a part with sardonic humour? His test will be: which gives the greater pain—belief or disbelief? Many poets break under the strain:

TO BEGUILE AND BETRAY

To beguile and betray, though pardonable in women,
Slowly quenches the divine need-fire
By true love kindled in them. Have you not watched
The immanent Goddess fade from their brows
When they make private to their mysteries
Some whip-scarred rogue from the hulks, some painted clown
From the pantomime—and afterwards accuse you
Of jealous hankering for the mandalot
Rather than horror and sick foreboding
That she will never return to the same house?

Convinced of her need for his love, the obsessed poet refuses to break under the strain; though at last realizing that Lyceia meant all she said at their first encounter: her beauty is her own, and she offers nothing but envy, hope and chagrin. Unlike Enkidu, he does not reproach the Goddess with her treacheries, but reads them as just criticism of his desire to possess her, and continues to love her selflessly:

EXPECT NOTHING

Give, ask for nothing, hope for nothing,
Subsist on crumbs, though scattered casually
Not for you (she smiles) but for the birds.
Though only a thief's diet, it staves off
Dire starvation, nor does she grow fat
On the bread she crumbles, while the lonely truth
Of love is honoured, and her pledged word.

Satisfied by this fresh evidence of her power, she softens towards him for awhile; though her eventual function and fate is to betray him, and thus forfeit the glory with which he enshrined her:

INTIMATIONS OF THE BLACK GODDESS

This they know well: the Goddess yet abides.
Though each new lovely woman whom she rides,
Straddling her neck a year or two or three,
Should sink beneath such weight of majesty
And, groping back to humankind, gainsay
The healing power that whitened all her way
With a broad track of trefoil—leaving you,
Her chosen lover, ever again thrust through
With daggers, your purse rifled, your rings gone—
Nevertheless they call you to live on
To parley with the pure, oracular dead,
To hear the wild pack whimpering overhead,
To watch the moon tugging at her cold tides.
Woman is mortal woman. She abides.

Orpheus, in the Greek myth, was taught by the Triple
Muse not only to enchant men and wild beasts with his
lyre, but to make rocks and trees move and follow him in
a dance. According to a later myth, his wife Eurydice
(whom he had married after a visit to Egypt) was
assaulted by the pastoral god Aristaeus, trod on a serpent
as she fled, and died of its venomous bite. Orpheus then
boldly harrowed Hell, intent on fetching her back. There,
with his lyre, he charmed the Dog Cerberus, the ferry-
man Charon and the three Judges of the Dead, temporarily suspended the tortures of the damned, and even
persuaded Hades, God of Tartarus, to set Eurydice free.
Hades made one condition: that Orpheus must not look
behind him until she was safely home under the light of
the sun. . . . Eurydice followed him up through the dark
passages of Tartarus, guided by his lyre; and it was only
on reaching the sunlight that he turned to reassure himself of her presence—and lost her for ever.

This same Orpheus is said, by the mythographers, to
have denounced human sacrifice and preached that the

Sun was a nobler deity than the Moon—for which blasphemy a group of Moon-worshipping, cannibalistic Maenads tore him in pieces. The Triple Muse collected his mangled limbs and buried them at Leibethra, where nightingales afterwards sang more sweetly than anywhere else in the world. . . . His head, though attacked by a jealous serpent, continued singing and was laid up in a cave at Antissa, sacred to Dionysus, God of Enlightenment. There it prophesied so clearly and constantly that at last Apollo, finding his own oracles at Delphi, Gryneium and Clarus deserted by visitants, stood over the head, crying: 'Cease to interfere in my business! I have suffered you long enough.' At this, we are told, the head fell silent.

It may well be that, sometime during the second millennium B.C., a Libyo-Thracian (afterwards identified with Orpheus) visited Egypt and brought back a mystic Sun-cult which local Moon-worshippers opposed. Yet there is more to this myth than a kernel of history: Eurydice ('Wide Rule') was, in fact, not Orpheus's wife, but the Triple Muse herself—*Diana in the leavës green, Luna who so bright doth sheen, Proserpina in Hell*, as John Skelton calls her.

Proserpina, or Persephone ('Voice of Destruction'), is the Muse in her most implacable aspect; and we know from the Demeter myth that Persephone, although carried off with a great show of unwillingness by Hades, a Serpent-god, soon broke her hunger strike in Tartarus by eating food of the dead, namely seven pomegranate seeds. As a result, she was ordered by Almighty Zeus to spend seven months of the year (or, some say, three) in Hades's company, but the remainder on earth. This can, of course, be read as a simple nature myth of winter's inclemency—pomegranates being the last fruit to ripen in Greece—and the return of spring, when Persephone's *Anthesterion*, or Flower Festival, was annually celebrated. Yet it yields a different sense when related to the Orpheus story.

Orpheus recognized and glorified the Muse; in gratitude, she lent him her own magical powers, so that he made trees dance—'trees', in ancient Europe, being a widely used metaphor of the poetic craft. Later, in Egypt, he learned a new solar perfectionism, which she rejected as foreign to her nature. How could Orpheus hope to keep her always beside him in the bright upper air of love and truth? Had she not a secret passion for serpents, a delight in murder, a secret craving for corpse flesh, a need to spend seven months of the year consorting with the sly, the barren, the damned? She might cherish Orpheus while still on earth, even calling him beautiful—since his beauty reflected her own—and mourn him when he was murdered. . . . Yet she could not be bound by his hopes for her perfectibility. Eurydice never trod accidentally on a serpent while avoiding Aristaeus's lustful embraces: she surely chose to couple with a serpent—as Mother Eurynome ('Wide Order'), her ancestress, herself had coupled with the world-snake Ophion. Simple-minded Orpheus flattered her pride by challenging death in his descent to Hell, and she pretended to follow him up into the sunlight. . . . But soon retired. He waited awhile at the entrance of the Taenaran Cave, keeping his back to it; then turned about and saw himself deceived once more:

FOOD OF THE DEAD

Blush as you stroke the curves—chin, lips and brow—
Of your scarred face,. Prince Orpheus: for she has called it
Beautiful, nor would she stoop to flattery.
Yet are you patient still, when again she has eaten
Food of the dead, seven red pomegranate seeds,
And once more warmed the serpent at her thighs
For a new progress through new wards of hell?

Arabs, when down-trodden, robbed or cheated, often refrain from curses, since these are apt to boomerang back. They merely cry instead: '*Moghreb, moghreb, moghreb!*', which means 'I am oppressed, I am oppressed, I am oppressed!' and leaves the avenging of their injury, if undeserved, to God or Fate. So should the poet refrain from cursing Eurydice, however ill she has used him:

EURYDICE

'*I am oppressed, I am oppressed, I am oppressed*'—
Once I utter the curse, how can she rest:
No longer able, weeping, to placate me
With renewed auguries of celestial beauty?

Speak, fly in her amber ring; speak, horse of gold!
What gift did I ever grudge her, or help withhold?
In a mirror I watch blood trickling down the wall—
Is it mine? Yet still I stand here proud and tall.

Look where she shines with a borrowed blaze of light
Among the cowardly, faceless, lost, unright,
Clasping a naked imp to either breast—
Am I not oppressed, oppressed, three times oppressed?

She has gnawn at corpse-flesh till her breath stank,
Paired with a jackal, grown distraught and lank,
Crept home, accepted solace, but then again
Flown off to chain truth back with an iron chain.

My own dear heart, dare you so war on me
As to strangle love in a mad perversity?
Is ours a fate that can ever be forsworn
Though my lopped head sing to the yet unborn?

Orpheus was torn in pieces: the fate of all Muse-worshipping poets. But his head continued to sing; and even the cynical Serpent (who asks: 'Why deceive yourself? She will always need corpse flesh and the charm of my subtle tongue') could not silence it. Neither could Apollo, God of Reason, make Orpheus hold his peace for ever. In the Palestinian myth of the rival twins, Aliyan and Mot, the Goddess Anatha lured first one, then the other, to her bed—murdering each in turn. Mot was the demi-god of drought, lack and evil. The Muse, in fact, alternates between the worlds of good and evil, plenty and lack; and her poet will have his head torn off and his limbs gnawn by greedy teeth if he attempts to change her. Yet still he believes that, one day, Eurydice must mount into the everlasting Garden of Paradise which she planted, and there make him her sole lover:

A LAST POEM

A last poem, and a very last, and yet another—
O, when can I give over?
Must I drive the pen until blood bursts from my nails
And my breath fails and I shake with fever,
Or sit well wrapped in a many-coloured cloak
Where the moon shines new through Castle Crystal?
Shall I never hear her whisper softly:
'But this is truth written by you only,
And for me only; therefore, love, have done'?

A poet who elects to worship Ishtar-Anatha-Eurydice, concentrates in himself the emotional struggle which has torn mankind apart: that futile war for dominance waged between men and women on battle-fields of the patriarchal marriage bed. He rejects the crude, self-sufficient male intelligence, yet finds the mild, complaisant Vesta insufficient for his spiritual needs. Renascent primitive woman, the White Goddess, to whom he swears allegiance, treats him no less contemptuously than she does anyone else in this man-ruled world; as in a race riot the colour of one's face is all that counts. . . . There can be no kindness between Ishtar and Enkidu, between Muse and poet, despite their perverse need for each other. Nor does a return to Vesta's gentle embraces—though he may never have denied her his affection—solve his problem. Marriage does not satisfy the physiological and emotional needs of more than one couple in ten.

Nevertheless Ishtar, though the most powerful deity of her day, did not rule alone. At Hierapolis, Jerusalem and Rome she acknowledged a mysterious sister, the Goddess of Wisdom, whose temple was small and unthronged. Call her the Black Goddess: Provençal and Sicilian 'Black Virgins' are so named because they derive from an ancient tradition of Wisdom as Blackness. This Black Goddess, who represents a miraculous certitude in love, ordained that the poet who seeks her must pass uncomplaining through all the passionate ordeals to which the White Goddess may subject him.

The *Orphic Fragments* tell how Night mothered a Love-god named Phanes, who set the Universe in motion. Night, for the Orphics, appeared in triad as Blackness (namely, Wisdom), Order and Justice. Before her cave sat the inescapable Rhea—the White Goddess—beating a brazen drum and compelling man's attention to Night's oracles. Throughout the Orient, Night was regarded as a positive power, not as a mere absence of daylight; and Black as a prime colour, not as absence of colour, was prized for capturing the Sun's virtue more than any other.

This myth surely needs no gloss? The Provencal and Sicilian Black Virgins are Sufic in origin—Perso-Arabic applications to Christian doctrine of the same ancient myth. The Virginal St Sophia—that is, Wisdom— mothers the creative Love-god:

INTIMATIONS OF THE BLACK GODDESS

THAT OTHER WORLD

Fatedly alone with you once more
As before Time first creaked:
Sole woman and sole man.

Others admire us as we walk this world:
We show them kindliness and mercy,
So be it none grow jealous
Of the truth that echoes between us two,
Or of that other world, in the world's cradle,
Child of your love for me.

In the Jewish Wisdom-cult, also apparently of Orphic origin, seven pillars are set up to support Wisdom's shrine: namely, the seven planetary powers of the seven-branched Candlestick. And when the Shunemite bride, whom Solomon in his wisdom adored, says in the *Canticles*: 'I am black, but comely,' her meaning is: 'Though comely, I am as wise as any crone.' She adds, half-humorously: 'The Sun has looked upon me.' And the Orphics, seekers after Wisdom like Hebrews and Sufis, chose the Sun as their metaphor of illumination.

Night had a dove's head, and Phanes, God of Love, was hatched from a silver egg that she laid. There is no more ancient emblem of love than the turtle-dove; or of spiritual re-birth than the phoenix. Shakespeare's strange prophetic line *The Phoenix and the turtle fled in a mutual flame from hence*, carries a world of meaning. The phoenix, according to the Egyptians, was born as a worm from the ashes of its self-consumed predecessor and, after four years, grew to a chick:

THE HEARTH

Here it begins: the worm of love breeding
Among red embers of a hearth-fire,
Turns to a chick, is slowly fledged,
And will hop from lap to lap in a ring
Of eager children basking at the blaze.

But the luckless man who never sat there,
Nor borrowed live coals from the sacred source
To warm a hearth of his own making,
Nor bedded lay under pearl-grey wings
In dutiful content,

How shall he watch at the stroke of midnight
Dove become phoenix, plumed with green and gold?
Or be caught up by jewelled talons
And haled away to a fastness of the hills
Where an unveiled woman, black as Mother Night,
Teaches him a new degree of love
And the tongues and songs of birds?

Poetry, it may be said, passes through three distinct
stages: first, the poet's introduction, by Vesta, to love in
its old-fashioned forms of affection and companionship;
next, his experience of death and recreation at the White
Goddess's hand; and lastly a certitude in love, given him
by the Black Goddess, his more-than-Muse.

The Black Goddess is so far hardly more than a word of
hope whispered among the few who have served their
apprenticeship to the White Goddess. She promises a
new pacific bond between men and women, correspond-
ing to a final reality of love, in which the patriarchal
marriage bond will fade away. Unlike Vesta, the Black
Goddess has experienced good and evil, love and hate,
truth and falsehood in the person of her sister; but chooses
what is good: rejecting serpent-love and corpse flesh.
Faithful as Vesta, gay and adventurous as the White
Goddess, she will lead man back to that sure instinct of
love which he long ago forfeited by intellectual pride.

It is idle to speculate what poets will then become, or
whether the same woman can, in fact, by a sudden
spectacular change in her nature, play two diverse parts
in one lifetime. Everything is possible. The Black
Goddess may even appear disembodied rather than

incarnate. . . . Does it matter? Poets, at any rate, will no longer be bullied into false complacency by the submissive sweetness of Vesta, or be dependent on the unpredictable vagaries of Anatha-Ishtar-Eurydice.

Lucid, dogmatic, liberal, infuriating, but always brilliant and delightful in their presentation, these eight pieces cover as wide a range as the interests of Robert Graves himself—from poetry and women to money and the qualities of magic—and hence his title for this book, joining two deities that stand in extreme opposition. All save one began as lectures during Mr. Graves' most recent trips to the United States and Great Britain:

Mammon is an engaging, informal discussion that traces the origins and history of money and touches on what it has meant in the author's own life.

Nine Hundred Iron Chariots speaks in praise of magic over science, comparing the poet and the scientist and finding the latter wanting.

Some Instances of Poetic Vulgarity is Mr. Graves at his sharply critical best, as he attacks phoniness in all guises and takes a hard look at some of the verse of Browning, Byron, Kipling, Thomas Campbell, and Swinburne.

(continued on back flap)